A CONNOISSEUR'S
GUIDE TO ANTIQUE
JEWELLERY

A CONNOISSEUR'S GUIDE TO ANTIQUE

JEWELLERY

RONALD PEARSALL

TODTRI

This book was designed and produced by TODTRI Book Publishers
P.O. Box 572, New York, NY 10116-0572
Fax: (212) 695-6984
e-mail: todtri@mindspring.com

Printed and bound in Singapore

ISBN 1-57717-152-7

Visit us on the web!
www.todtri.com

Author: Ronald Pearsall

Publisher: Robert M. Tod
Editor: Nicolas Wright
Art Directorr: Ron Pickless
Typesetting & DTP: Blanc Verso UK

CONTENTS

INTRODUCTION

The urge to beautify the person dates from pre-history. It can be done by tattooing, scarifying and, above all, by attaching decorative materials. The ancient Incas pierced the ear-lobes of youths at puberty, inserted plaques of gold, resulting in enormous ears. Other nations pierced the nose or lips and inserted horizontal bars of wood, metal or bone. But it was more common to suspend objects, whether natural or custom made. Thus the genesis of jewellery.

The wearing of jewellery is not necessarily vanity. Jewellery is worn to transform and heighten the personality, to raise the status of the wearer, and talismanic and occult powers have often been ascribed to gemstones. This was especially true of the first of the great jewel-using civilizations, that of ancient Egypt, where jewellery of the highest technical quality was made using methods not dissimilar to those employed today. Many gemstones were found in the desert around the Nile Valley – cornelian, jasper, rock-crystal, agate, amethyst, chalcedony, chrysoprase, felspar, garnet, and nephrite(jade). Turqouise was highly esteemed, but involved mining in remote Sinai. Lapis lazuli had to be imported from as far afield as Afghanistan, where there were only two mountains containing lapis lazuli (both of which are mined today).

Throughout the ages and in almost every country, jewellery has long been prized, as much for its intrinsic beauty as for its monetary value. Its decorative and adornment qualities have never been in doubt. The expression "a diamond is forever" is a truism which will last as long as the object itself.

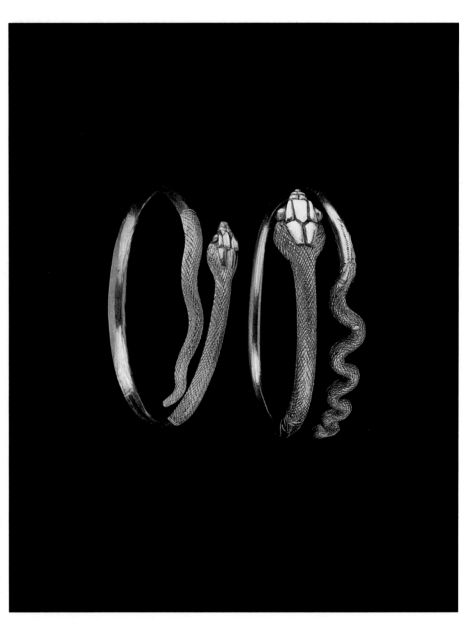

Above: Romano-Egyptian bracelets in the form of a snake dating from the first century AD. The snake bracelet has proved an enduring form to this day.

Opposite: A magnificent piece of Minoan gold jewellery from the Bronze Age culture of the Mediterranean island of Crete, around 3000 BC to 1100 BC.

EARLY JEWELLERY

The colour of the stones used by the ancients had magical properties – red for flesh, green for growth, and blue to counter the evil eye – thus the special appeal of the blazing blue of lapis lazuli. Gold was more common than silver, and expertly crafted to show off the gemstones. Silver had to be mined, gold was found, freed from rock by erosion over the ages, carried down mountain sides, and ending up as dust on the beds of streams or compounded with sand to form

nuggets. Discoveries in the nineteenth century and the finding of the tomb of Tutankhamun in 1922 provided evidence of the sophistication of the Egyptian culture, and its skills with gold. Besides golden thrones, golden beds and the golden sarcophagus that held Tutankhamun's remains the royal jewels were buried with him, set with turquoise, lapis lazuli and cornelian, worn to propitiate the gods (perpetuated in marriage rings, papal rings, the tradition of birthstones and jewellery made in the form of the signs of the zodiac).

The intact jewels of five Egyptian princesses from about 2400 BC were discovered in 1894-5, giving an insight into everyday jewellery of the period. It is evident that the full possibilities of gold were known – that a single ounce could be beaten wafer thin and produce 100 square feet of gold leaf, that an ounce of gold can produce 50 miles of wire. Gold symbolised the sun god Ra and as the kings of Egypt believed they were his descendants they laid claim to all the gold in their lands. Criminals, slaves and captives were sent to work the great mines in the plateau bordering the Red Sea or tunnel for it in the rich deposits in Nubia.

Other ancient civilizations which possessed little or no gold or trivial quantities imported it from Egypt. The quest for gold was often a reason for war. When Alexander conquered Persia he appropriated all its gold. The excavations in the nineteenth century by Heinrich

Above: A Greek hollow gold bracelet from about the third century BC. The Greeks inherited the marvellous skills of the Egyptian goldsmiths and jewellers, and built upon them.

Opposite: Types of jewellery were not restricted to certain countries, and most were universal. Consequently there is some difficulty in assigning antique jewellery. The two ancient gold bracelets are accompanied by a Greek gold sheet disc. Gold was more common than silver, much of it imported from Egypt which had large deposits in Nubia.

Overleaf: A selection of ancient jewellery. The skills of the early craftsmen in gems and precious metals have never been excelled, and the only true advance since antiquity has been the ability to cut diamonds.

*Above: Medallions associated with
Alexander the Great of Macedon.*

Schliemann on the site of what he believed to be the classical city of Troy uncovered great quantities of gold jewellery, superbly fashioned, sometimes geometric, sometimes naturalistic featuring animal, bird, and human forms – grasshoppers, mythical griffins (upper part eagle, lower part lion), stags, doves – the list is endless. There were also daggers and other weapons illustrated with hunting scenes, carried out with great vigour and authority. All the techniques of the goldsmith were utilised. Unlike many types of antiques where there is so often a history of progress as new techniques are discovered, jewellery only changed (often for the worse) rather than developed.

The types of articles made were those with which we are familiar today – bracelets, necklaces, rings, brooches, hair decorations, whether tiaras or less formal pieces. Some jewellery was perforated so that it could be sewn on dresses. Women's jewellery depended – and still does – largely on what they wore, what cosmetics they favoured, and what their life styles were. Clothing was plain, women did not consider it necessary to cover their breasts, and they rarely wore footwear. With the exception of coloured trailing bands and garlands, worn for festive occasions, the use of head coverings was restricted to the ruling class. A gold collar worn on the head was a token of power. Women enhanced the look of their eyes and brows with black and wore green eyeshadow.

Both men and women wore jewellery in ancient Egypt, the women wearing artifical flowers as well. Necklaces and bracelets, worn both above and below the elbow, were especially popular. The practice of burial with jewellery was practised throughout the civilized world – Babylon, Assyria, Persia, Phoenicia, Etrusca, Rome and the Greek states.

The gemstones used at the time were mostly those with which we are acquainted today, though there was not the division between precious stones and the semi-precious. Certain precious stones such as rubies had been mined in Burma since prehistoric times and were not known in the centres of civilization in the Middle East except by accident. Gemstones were valued more by their size and meaning than their quality. Most stones could be cut, but the art of facetting (providing flat surfaces to increase the sparkle) was not fully exploited.

There is a strong family relationship between the jewellery found in the eastern Mediterranean countries, one of the reasons being that trading links were strong. Where jewellery has been excavated there is no evidence that it was actually made in that country. The skilled jewellers also moved from country to country, bringing in their own motifs. The word country is also somewhat misleading; there were few formal borders, and there were centres of power rather than states.

What is also evident is the influence, independence and power of the women. They had a penchant for "cuteness", as can be seen in the tiny animal and bird motifs on their jeweller., They also had a strong sense of their own beauty and how it could be enhanced. When men tried to increase their status they could seem comic; beards were highly favoured in ancient Egypt, to the extent that those who probably could not grow them wore false ones. It is also clear that modesty, as we know it, was unknown. Nakedness, both in men and women, was commonplace, especially evident among the Greeks.

Certain civilizations did have their individual characteristics. One of the greatest of the civilizations, with its own marvellous mythology, was the Cretan (Minoan), and here society was dominated by women.

Above: An earring from Perugia in Etruria, part of what became Italy. The Etruscans were an advanced people, coming from the east in the twelfth century BC. They declined in the fifth and fourth centuries BC following invasions from Rome and by the Gauls. They spoke a non-Indo-European language which has never been deciphered.

Above: This jewellery from Peru features the condor, which enjoyed a major role in South American myth.

Opposite: A selection of rings, including a late Roman silver-gilt ring inscription, a Roman or Byzantine gold intaglio ring (a design engraved or carved so that it is below the surface) depicting a male portrait head, a further Roman intaglio ring and a heavy gold ring. When Rome collapsed, Byzantium became the cultural centre of the world.

Overleaf: A selection of ancient Egyptian jewellery. Jewellery was extensively worn by both men and women, and most of the gemstones we are acquainted with were used, including the magic lapis lazuli from Afghanistan.

The snake priestess in her modish costume, with breasts uncovered, who is known to us through a small ceramic figure from Knossos and dating from the seventeenth century BC epitomises with her wasp waist and flounced skirt the Minoan civilization. Minoan culture spread to Mycenae, the scene of the excavations of Troy, and Mycenae in the north-eastern Peloponnese eventually predominated. The women of Crete, pleasure-loving and sophisticated, wore the entire range of jewellery – rings, necklaces, ear-rings, diadems, slides, pendants and decorative pins. The jewellers were masters in the manipulation of precious metals; the favoured gemstones were steatite, agate, porphyry, amethyst and jasper.

With the collapse of Mycenae, the jewellers and skilled craftsmen moved to Greece, adapting to the slightly changing demands of the most advanced culture of all time, though there were few dramatic innovations as the manufacture of jewellery had reached a peak of perfection, and the range of gemstones was well known. Clothing was different in Greece, and thus the jewellery pieces needed to fit in with changing costume. In archaic Greece the standard garment of both men and women was a rectangular woollen cloth draped around the

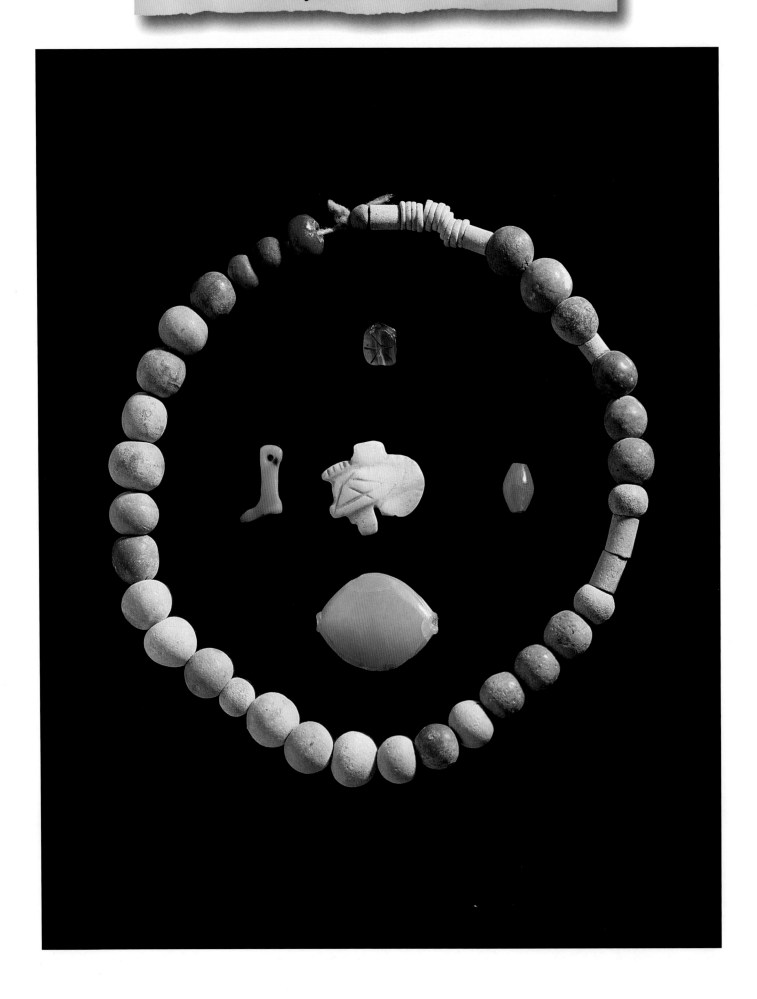

body, called the chlaina for men and the peplos for women. A short cloak was worn over the peplos, which was open at one side and its wearers were known as "women who show their hips". The chiton was introduced from the east, a type of tunic, draped, later girded at the waist to form a sort of blouse. Underwear was not worn (unlike in Egypt where men and women wore loin cloths). In cold weather the himation (a large chlaina or peplos) was worn, often over the head forming a hood. The chlamys was a knee-length himation worn by youths and soldiers.

Below: A gold necklace from Syria, perhaps from the time when the Phoenicians who lived there and in Lebanon were the prime trading nation of the world.

Greek women loved jewellery and trinkets, including toe-rings as well as the familiar bracelets, pins, and necklaces. Footwear was not worn indoors. The jewellery is distinguished by the skilled use of fretwork and excavations have uncovered great quantities of discs of gold, often with an embossed centre, sometimes with accessories dangling from them. The Greek civilization lasted many centuries; there was a period c 600 BC to c 475 BC when gold was scarce and substitute bronze and silver have rarely survived. Besides traditional gemstones amber was much used, especially by the Romans, mostly imported from the Baltic, and glass beads, developed by the Egyptians, were rated as highly as gemstones. Amber was believed to have healing and magical powers, and was used as amulets as well as for decorative inlays.

The classic period of Greek jewellery was 475 BC to 330 BC. Among the most spectacular pieces were wreaths worn by victors at games made of gold, silver, gilded wood and bronze and faithfully imitating myrtle and olive wreaths. Ear-rings included spirals with the thin end passing through the ear-lobe and the other end ornamented with human or animal heads. Disc-shaped ear studs were often worn. Necklaces of melon or egg-shaped

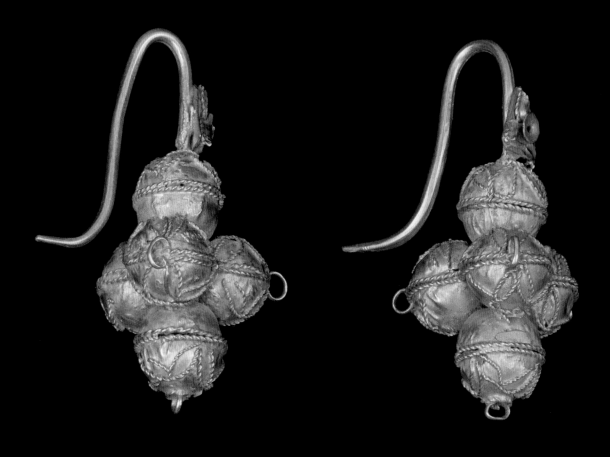

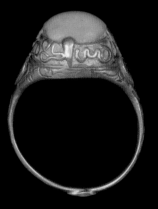

Left: Persian jewellery of the golden age, the twelfth and thirteenth centuries AD, when the Persians were a great civilization. They had access to the rubies of India and Burma, rare in the ancient civilizations a thousand years earlier.

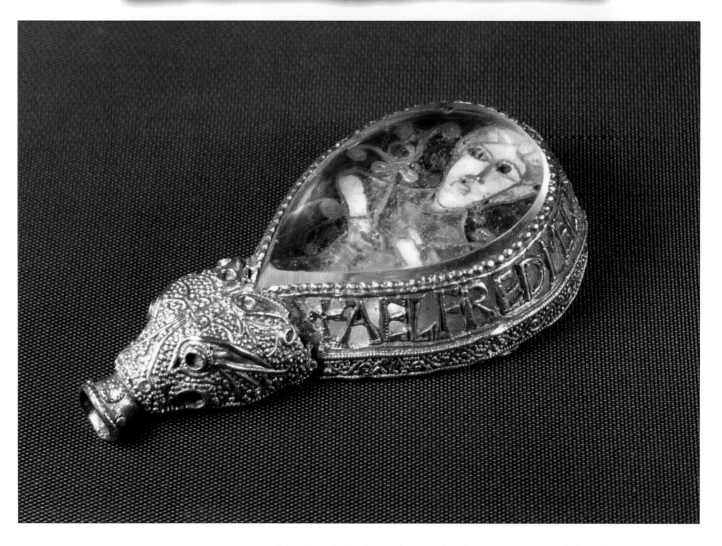

Above: The famous Alfred Jewel, of gold, rock crystal and enamel, of great intricacy, and dating back to the ninth century AD.

golden beads had pendants of palmettes or animal heads. Bracelets were sometimes left incomplete, the open ends decorated with animal heads, and spiral snake bracelets were a long-lived type which never, even to this day, have gone out of fashion. Pins of gold or bronze with heads depicting pine-cones, hearts, bees, and other motifs were worn in pairs, one on each shoulder, sometimes linked by a chain. Fibulae (brooches with pins) were not too popular in Greece but were in Italy. Rings of all kinds were worn, signet rings, rings set with stones, including lately discovered topaz and garnet, and rings with stones carved into the shape of the Egyptian scarab beetle, one of the most potent of all symbols. These often swivelled to reveal a flat lower surface carved with a device used as a seal. New techniques were introduced including the use of a cutting wheel and a drill so that hard stones such as cornelian could be carved .

Etruria was on the west coast of Italy; but no-one quite knows where the Etruscans came from. They evolved a new technique, the granulation of surfaces, practised with incomparable skill and remaining a puzzle until the nineteenth century when gold-workers in the Abruzzi were found to have had the skills passed down to them. They were persuaded to go to Naples, and examples of their work were shown at the London Exhibition of 1872. Granulation is a process in which minute grains of gold are arranged in patterns and soldered on to a back-

ground with copper carbonate mixed with water and fish glue.

Little distinguishes Etruscan from Greek jewellery and with the increasing supremacy of Rome Greek craftsmen moved across the Adriatic. Technical developments, such as the evolution of a round-headed drill, had an adverse effect on design. It was easier to make jewellery, but precision was occasionally lost. During the Roman Republic ostentation was frowned upon, but under the emperors jewellers had complete freedom. Emeralds from new Egyptian mines were used as well as aquamarines, pearls, and sapphires. Uncut diamonds now appeared, but were too hard to cut, and it would be nearly 2000 years before other than a round-headed diamond was possible. Jewellery was made throughout the Roman Empire. Jet from Whitby in England found its way to Rome, just as Roman jewellery spread over the western world.

The great contribution of the Romans to jewellery was the cameo, cutting away the top surface of a stone to reveal darker shades below, used for bracelets, rings and pendants. Another innovation was the setting into rings of coins. Bronze and iron rings sometimes have a small key attached, probably to unlock a dactyliotha or cabinet of rings or women's jewel-boxes. The diadem (tiara) is rare in Roman jewellery. Hair-pins in great variety were common as hair styles were luxuriant, and ear-rings of the circular and S- types were popular,

Above: Chest ornament with solar and lunar symbols from the tomb of Tutenkhamun.

21

Above: A display of ancient Egyptian jewellery. Thanks to the ceremonies of ritual burial much Egyptian jewellery has survived.

often with suspended pearls and glass beads.

As the Roman civilization drew to an end there was an increased emphasis on multi-coloured jewellery with different coloured stones used in one piece, a degree of flashiness that denotes decadence. It seemed that the craft of jewellery had reached its limits. The centre of power moved to Byzantium (Constantinople); Constantine the Great (306 – 337) was the creator of the "Christian Roman Empire", and Byzantium reached its peak in the ninth and tenth centuries, declining in the thirteenth.

Early Byzantine jewellery was Roman in influence, but Persian and Arabic influences made themselves felt and costume and jewellery became more opulent, especially among the high ranking. Heavy decorated clothing was worn, shot through with gold and large areas were covered with pearls and precious stones. The stiff formality of clothing, which was all-enveloping both for men and women, was in stark contrast to the airy costume of Greece and Rome.

During the so-called Dark Ages, Roman prototypes were amended and transformed, both amongst the Germanic tribes and the Celts, though the Celtic group had a long and independent line of descent. This produced hammered work with details in repousse, the use of coloured enamels, amber, and rounded-cut rock crystal and in design the use of intertwining curves and naturalistic detail in spirit far removed from that of the ancient world. In aesthetic appeal it was

Above: Although Egyptian everyday costume was simple, men and women displayed jewellery in abundance. Rings, bracelets, necklaces - all the present forms were used.

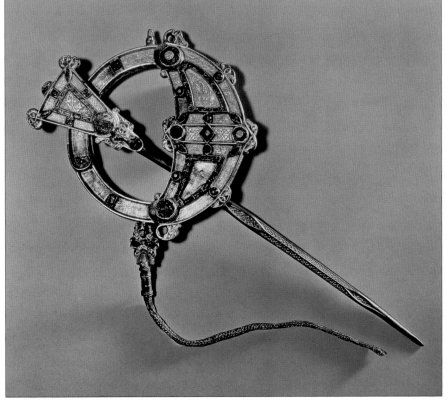

Left: During the Dark Ages when the civilizing influences of Rome were fast disappearing, Celtic jewellery, based on spirals and natural forms not seen again until the art nouveau movement, provides an indication that all was not lost. This is the Tara brooch, named after the seat of the ancient kings of Ireland, dating from the eighth century.

nearer to the marvellous jewellery of the art nouveau period in the late nineteenth and early twentieth than the power jewellery of the Renaissance and after.

Although the nations of the east shared the desire for self-adornment, attitudes towards jewellery was very different. In the west, natural supplies of precious metals and gemstones were limited; in the east, they were in abundance, and this determined the way they were used. In India there was little attention paid to beautifying a single gem by cutting and cherishing it. Gemstones were worn in abundance by both men and women, sometimes set in enamels in a lac-like substance. As in the west, there were proscriptions on who could wear jewellery; in India, lower castes for forbidden to adorn themselves, and those who were allowed to wear jewellery were not permitted to wear it below the waist.

In China there was a reluctance to meddle with the earth's treasures and gold was sparingly used. Particularly in India, gemstones were recycled to conform to new fashions and little survives earlier than the eighteenth century. This is true also of western jewellery, though many of the great pieces were preserved. However, much of it has been lost for ever.

Above: A selection of gold jewellery of about the twelfth century, a period of great contrasts. Magnificence, such as the cathedrals, and mediocrity with artefacts hardly developed since the Dark Ages..

Opposite: A pair of Persian gold bracelets of the twelfth century, a silver and niello (a black composition for filling in) amulet of the same date, and a somewhat later Persian silver crescent amulet.

GEMSTONES

There is more myth, legend, superstition and awe concerning the diamond than all other gemstones put together. It is the hardest of all natural substances and is one of the few gemstones to be of any practical use, as a cutting tool. As early as the sixth century in India the perfect diamond was described. It should have six sharp points, eight very flat and similar sides, and twelve straight and sharp edges. It was described but rarely found, as until the fifteenth century knowledge of how to facet them was imperfect. Only Brahmins were allowed to possess pure colourless diamonds. Few good diamonds left India for the west before about AD 1000. The Chinese were not interested in the aesthetic qualities of diamonds, only in their cutting ability and their mystical overtones.

Probably the "table-cut" diamond originated in India, originally, with Borneo, the main providers of diamonds, but until diamonds were faceted they were regarded as less valuable than rubies and emeralds. They were also found in large quantities; in the Indian Golconda mines in 1661 the work force was around 60,000. After sixteen hundred years of mining, the Indian diamonds dried up, but an alternative source was discovered in Brazil in 1730, and when this began to fail the South African mines were discovered in 1867. Unlike their predecessors De Beers Consolidated Mines employed heavy machinery; for every one-carat diamond discovered five tons of rock have to be dug, moved, sorted and processed. A carat is 1/142 of an ounce. Africa produces 97% of the world's diamonds.

When the full beauty of the diamond was demonstrated by cutting it became beyond value. Especially if it was large. A diamond weigh-

Above: The Russians were masters of jewellery and precious metals, and this lavish diamond spray of about 1760 was once owned by Catherine the Great (1729 - 1796) and was part of the Russian crown jewels.

Opposite: A diamond, enamel and gold pendant.

Above: A Renaissance gold, enamel and pearl pendant in the form of a ram, with added rubies.

ing 1680 carats was sent to the court of Portugal. It was valued by one expert at £224 million, by another at £3.5 million.

Catherine the Great of Russia offered £104,166 for a diamond of 193 carats, and it eventually found its way into the sceptre of the Russian royal family. Perhaps the most famous diamond of all is the Kohinoor, dating back to at least 1304, presented to Queen Victoria. It originally weighed nearly 800 carats, but was incompetently recut into a brilliant of 108 carats. It was the central stone in the crown made for the coronation of Queen Elizabeth (now the Queen Mother) in 1937 and forms part of the British Crown Jewels.

Since the mines of South Africa were worked, the largest diamonds have come from there. The most famous is the Cullinan, a diamond of 3,106 metric carats found in Transvaal in 1905, presented to King Edward VII of England, and cut in Amsterdam into nine main gemstones, the four largest being incorporated in the British Crown Jewels.

A fine diamond is pure carbon. One atom of nitrogen in a hundred thousand atoms of carbon give a yellowish tinge and is thus much less valuable, though in a combination hardly noticed. Because most dia-monds are so tiny they are mostly, with the exception of rings, used in an ensemble. A completely flawless diamond (a diamond without internal faults) is rare – one in 800. Cutters can be unscrupulous; to keep a diamond over the magic weight of one carat they will make the pavilion (the bottom) of the diamond unnecessarily deep (reducing the brilliance). A diamond may be a girl's best friend but she has to have her wits about her.

High-quality coloured diamonds are rare. The celebrated Hope Diamond is blue. One in 100,000 diamonds can be described as a "fine, fancy coloured diamond", and most came from the lost mines of India, but off-colour diamonds can be confused initially with other gemstones. Diamonds can also be mistaken for imitations, either honest or fraudulent. Paste can be a substitute for any gem, but it is predominantly used for diamond lookalikes. Known on the continent as Stras, Strass, or Strasse, even today, named after a Strasbourg jeweler, it dates from about 1732, and was very fashionable. Paste is glass. Zircon, a diamond substitute, is a natural gemstone, given its name in 1794.

Diamonds, rubies, emeralds and sapphires are the precious stones; the rest are semi-precious. These are labels of convenience, formerly haphazardly based on the hardness of the gems though inconsistent, becoming gradually discarded, and owe much to fashion and rarity. Rarity fluctuates as new deposits are found and opal could be considered rare until vast deposits were discovered in Australia. Opaline is imitation opal. Of the precious stones other than diamonds, rubies are the rarest and carry the most kudos; although of the same group as emeralds, differing owing in the introduction of naturally occurring chemical colour-changing factors. They are approximately three times more valuable.

Mostly mined in Burma and Thailand, rubies were largely inaccessible to the ancient world and thus had the mystery of the unknown. The sapphire enjoyed much of the same prestige, as Sri Lanka was the primary source, a faraway place difficult to access. In England in the fourteenth century every bishop taking office was presented with a sapphire ring as it epitomized heaven, sapphire being mentioned in the Bible. For a brief period pearls enjoyed the same esteem as they were first discovered only in the Persian Gulf. Although other sources were found when they were artificially produced (the cultured pearl) the status of the pearl dropped dramatically (and the price – resulting in the Great Pearl Crash of 1930).

Above: A diamond, emerald and enamel necklace.

Right: Jet from Whitby had been used by the Romans, but it received a great boost when it was used as mourning jewellery after the death of Queen Victoria's husband in 1861. It was incorporated into everyday jewellery, as well as being used for mementoes and novelties, and this necklace, the earrings, brooches and the cross of about 1870 were typical of the undemanding products of this small Yorkshire town.

Above: The Hope diamond is blue. Only one diamond in 100,000 is a "fancy coloured" diamond, and most came from the lost mines of India.

Opposite: A carved jadeite - the hardest most valued kind of jade, coloured diamond, ruby and sapphire brooch in the form of a parrot by Carvin French.

Gems can have aesthetic appeal, be magical, be associative, or be representative of raw power. The princes of Burma decreed that any ruby weighing over six carats was the property of the royal household and any miner who did not surrender a large ruby was put to death. The miners countered this by smashing up the large rubies. There is rarely a free market in gems, which are often hemmed in with proscriptions, and are manipulated according to the condition of the market, sometimes in extreme secrecy. A new find can throw the whole of the industry into confusion.

Fakes and imitations of gemstones abound. Many are genuine attempts to reproduce the real thing at a fraction of the cost with no intent to deceive and this has been done since ancient times, using coloured glass or ceramics. There is also the factor that some gemstones have close relations which are palmed off on the unknowing. This is particularly true of rubies and until the invention of scientific instruments such as the microscope and spectroscope garnets and spinels were frequently confused with rubies. In a reasonable world garnets and spinels would occupy the same plane as rubies, but jewellery does not live in a reasonable world. What is known as the Black Prince's ruby is a spinel, as is the enormous red stone in the crown of Catherine II of Russia made in 1762.

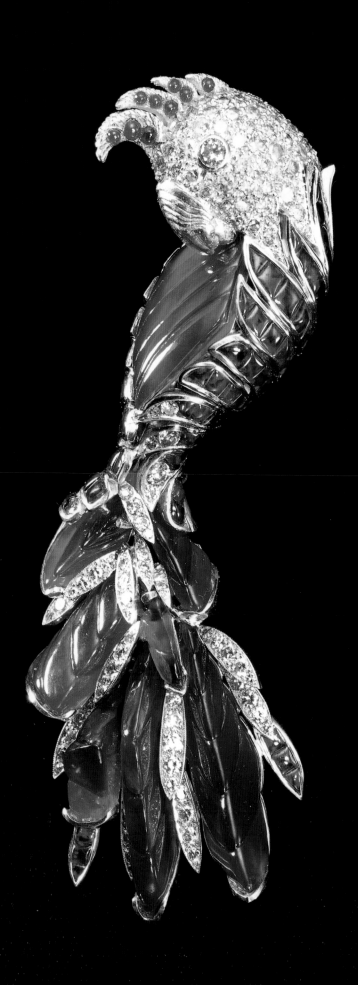

Synthetic gemstones have almost the same qualities as the genuine article, and their acceptance largely depends on habit and the prevailing culture. In Britain synthetics are shunned, in America they are accepted. Synthetic stones can have the same chemical and physical properties as the real thing and when offered at a reasonable price can be turned away as being too good to be true. This may be a temporary view as the supply of natural stones runs out. A Brazilian emerald mine employed 10,000 miners in the 1970s; by the 1980s the number was down to 1,500. Another element which may encourage the acceptance of synthetics is the cost of insurance for genuine stones, or the impossibility of getting insurance for stones that are worn rather than kept in a bank vault.

Synthetic stones were first produced in the nineteenth century – synthetic rubies are the jewels used in watches. In the 1930s emerald crystals were grown in a crucible at the chemical works of I.G. Farben in Germany, though not marketed at the time. After World War II they were produced in America. Man-made versions of opal, turquoise, alexandrite, ruby, and lapis lazuli were developed and made in France, and it is difficult to think of a stone which cannot be emulated.

Although rubies are characterized by a single colour, red, the reds come in all shades, the most sought after being "pigeon-blood", not a poetic metaphor, but the colour of the blood that appears in the

Above: A sapphire, diamond and enamel clip-on brooch in the form of a cicada. Insects were popular as brooch themes, as were flowers and birds, though nothing was prohibited, including trains and, from the Edwardian period, motor cars. The brooch was a fun item.

Opposite: Jewellery of the nineteenth century, a necklace with graduated ruby beads, an Indian enamel and crystal necklace and an Indian pearl and diamond choker. The choker was made fashionable by Alexandra, wife of King Edward VII, who, it is said, wore one to hide a scar.

Above: A pair of Indian Mogul emerald drop-ear pendants.

Opposite: An amethyst necklace with a matching diamond star brooch of the mid-nineteenth century. These partures could also include tiaras and other accessories.

nostrils of a freshly killed pigeon. Less than one in 22,000 rubies has this shade, and it is likely to have come from Burma. Size for size, it is the most valuable jewel including diamonds. In Sri Lanka rubies are pinkish and watery, not so highly prized. Thai rubies contain more iron and are inclined to the purply-brown and a newcomer from 1975, the Kenyan ruby, is even darker and browner than that from Thailand.

Ruby mines in Burma go back to prehistoric times. Between 1888 – 1931 the British ran them, and in the 1960s the supply of Burmese rubies began to dry up. The Sri Lankan mines were described by Marco Polo (1254 – 1324) and the rubies are largely alluvial, found by panning streams as with gold, though the central core of the ruby supply in the mountains has never been found.

Red spinels and garnets are distinguished from rubies by their shape and chemical make-up; ruby always crystallizes into a six-sided prism with flat faces. The others are diamond or lozenge shaped. The bigger rubies lie nearer the earth's surface, and it is doubtful whether any more large specimens will turn up. A new deposit was found in Greenland but turned out to be disappointing. As with diamonds, rubies were cut until the fifteenth century with a rounded top and no flat facets. All rubies contain flaws, which often contribute to the beauty of the stone and in certain rubies a flaw under a microscope can have the appearance of silk due to the presence of rutile (titanium oxide) needles. A skilled cutter can profit by this flaw and produce a "star" ruby, capitalizing on the reflections.

When gems were prized for their size and prestige, beauty was of less account, but with the increasing ability to provide facets, leading eventually to the "brilliant" 58-facet cut, large rubies set in crowns, book covers, daggers, and gold surrounds were removed and recut, making them considerably smaller but more lustrous. The original

Left: A convoluted turquoise and diamond
necklace of the nineteenth century which
looks as though it has been thrown together
rather than designed.

Above: A Victorian ruby and diamond tiara. Unlike some items of jewellery, tiaras came and went as fashion shifted, and in some cultures they were not known at all. The well-off Victorians wore everything that came their way.

stones were often replaced with imitations, so that in some cases a noble crown, assumed to be beyond price, can be hardly more than a theatre prop.

Rubies were probably more prized in India and the east than the west, and the Hindus called the ruby ratna raj, the king of stones. It was associated with love and also protected the wearer from wounds and cured haemorrhaging. John Ruskin, the Victorian art critic and voice of the nation, thought it "the loveliest precious stone of which I have any knowledge" but as his taste was famously faulty one cannot pay too much attention to his recommendation.

Emeralds were linked with Cleopatra and the emerald mine bearing her name near the Red Sea was rediscovered in 1818, containing hundreds of shafts running into the hillside, some penetrating 800 feet. Ancient tools date the mines to at least 1650 BC. It was the only known source of emeralds in the ancient world, though another source was later found in the Austrian mountains near Salzburg, probably discovered by the Romans. In the sixteenth century the Spaniards conquered Peru and took over the emerald mines; emeralds were also found by panning. As the Spaniards ceased mining for 200 years it is reasonable to assume that the supply ran out, though the

Peruvian mines were reopened during this century. The finest greens were found in emeralds from Colombia, the location of the mines being discovered by the Spanish through torture. Emeralds are notoriously heavily included (flawed) and a fair-sized emerald, clean and of good colour, is one of the most expensive of all gemstones. The Egyptians and the Romans imitated emeralds using pottery and glass. Flawed emeralds were treated by unscrupulous cutters with green oil to hide surface cracks. A less sophisticated method was painting the back of the stone with green pigment.

Emerald is a beryl, which is colourless. The green colour comes from the natural addition of chromium. Emeralds have also been found in India and Russia (from 1832) and in 1955 in Zimbabwe, initially enormously exciting, though the stones were small and after 20 years the supply began to run out. There were other finds in Zambia and Brazil, of modest quality, and even isolated finds in North Carolina. None of the emeralds found approaches those of Colombia, which were routinely sent to India for cutting.

Like the ruby, the sapphire is a corundum, and comes in a variety of colours but only blue or purply-blue are highly valued though the attractive pastel-coloured sapphires are less than a tenth of the price

Above: A 1930s ruby and diamond bracelet. The Art Deco period saw a rejection of the old categories of precious and semi-precious stones, and every conceivable material, including aluminium and plastics, were used in high-quality pieces.

of the blue. In the ancient world sapphires were supposed to protect the wearer from envy and from capture by enemies; it also represented peace. The majority of engagement rings today are sapphire and diamond. Small sapphires are cheap and plentiful, most coming from Australia, often with a greenish tinge and sometimes so dark that they look black in some lights. The finest sapphires come from Burma and Kashmir, exposed by an avalanche (or rock fall as there are several versions of the story) in 1881 and Sri Lanka. In the 1930s sapphires were discovered in Thailand, and new mines have opened in Cambodia and Africa, though the quality is watery or inky. Large sapphires are not uncommon – an American jeweller once owned one weighing 337 carats. Not many blue stones can be mistaken for sapphires with the exception of tanzanite. Sapphires are sometimes presented as "doublets" – two stones cemented together, the upper layer genuine, the lower synthetic, clearly intended to deceive as the use of a lens will confirm that the upper layer is genuine and the lower layer is not observable. Other stones are also made into doublets, or sometimes triplets.

The cream of the sapphire cutters are in Sri Lanka. Cutting sap-

Above: Modern jewellery from the personal collection of the Princess Salimah Aga Khan in emeralds and diamonds, made by Van Kleef and Arples probably about 1960.

Opposite: A selection of Victorian brooches of restrained appeal, a lapis lazuli brooch with Roman profiles, a spray of flowers brooch, a gold filigree, turquoise and pearl brooch, opal and diamond brooch, a lozenge-shape brooch, and diamond cluster bar brooch. All rather subdued in style and somewhat matronly.

phires is more demanding than with other gems, as blue sapphires comprise blue and purple and great skill is essential. Discussions between cutters on how to deal with a particular piece can last for months. Heat treatment can sometimes improve the colour. As with emeralds, traditional sapphire sources are running thin. There will therefore be an even more pronounced tendency to recycle antique gems and refashion them into a more modish form, traditional practice in the jewellery business.

To most people, especially those without foreknowledge, non-precious gems are visually on a par with emeralds, rubies and sapphires, and some are preferred. The cornelian necklace is the classic midldle-class piece of jewellery. Gemstones exist in geological families, and the beryl family includes both emeralds and aquamarines, a stone sacred to the Native Americans for whom it epitomises the sky. Unlike emeralds, aquamarines are often flawless, and, to the detriment of their market value, can be huge, a single crystal being five feet in height. Many aquamarines, particularly the small ones, are pale, and the most desirable are the larger darker specimens from Brazil. They are found world wide, but probably 80 per cent of aquamarines start up as green and are turned blue by heat treatment, a permanent process and not widely publicised.

The morganite is also a beryl, pale pink in colour and named after

Above: An unusual brooch in the form of a tortoise, using mother-of-pearl, turquoise, green garnets, and a gold setting, proof that the Victorians could produce first-rate jewellery.

Opposite: Lapis lazuli bead chain (rather than necklace), sapphire and diamond aigrettes (sprays of gems for the hair), a blue and yellow sapphire bracelet, a rose diamond and lapis lazuli flower-head brooch, and two black pearl rings.

Left: A diamond and pearl necklace, dating from the seventeenth century, with three beads inscribed with the names of Indian Mogul emperors. The Mogul dynasty was founded in 1526, was weakened by inter-dynastic wars in the eighteenth century, and was dissolved finally by the British in 1857.

the American banker J.P. Morgan who collected them presumably before they were named anything which must have been confusing. Found mostly in Brazil and the United States, morganites too are heat treated to get rid of a yellowish tinge. Pink topaz, kunzite, and pink sapphires are very similar in appearance. The only other beryl at all used extensively in jewellery is the heliodor, named after the Greek word for sun, and at its best golden yellow. Except for the emerald, the beryls have not been popular in the United Kingdom as ring stones, as good colour stones are too large for British tastes.

Garnets come in a variety of colours though only the red – also known as a carbuncle ("glowing coals") (though the term carbuncle can also indicate any stone where the back is carved out) – is well known or much used, first of all in the ancient world, then by warriors in the Dark Ages who introduced them to Britain. They were part of the treasure at Sutton Hoo (the site of a Saxon ship burial in Suffolk, England, dating from about AD 650, excavated in 1939). They were worn extensively throughout the ages and were much liked by the Victorians, especially if they were in quantity and could be presented in a composed group, the parure, a matched set of jewellery usually comprising necklace, bracelet, ear-rings and brooch, plus optional tiara (diadem), and buckle. A demi-parure is two items only. Items from a parure were sometimes multi-functional – the tiara could be dismantled and turned into a restrained head-band.

Above: An important sapphire ring. Sapphires belong to the upper echelons of the gem world, formerly only found in Sri Lanka. They had religious overtones and in the fourteenth century an emerald was presented to a newly consecrated bishop as it represented heaven.

Opposite: An extravagant Indian multi-strand pearl necklace, each strand suspending a series of tassels comprising emeralds, rubies, and pearls. India was rich in pearls, which thrived in the Persian Gulf which was for a time the main world supply.

Above: A collection of mourning jewellery from about 1850. Mourning was a never-ending process in the nineteenth century, as large families were the norm and the death rate from cholera and other diseases was high, and everyone was familiar with death. A complex mourning ceremony helped deal with the trauma.

Opposite: A modern selection of modern ruby and diamond jewellery signed by Van Cleef and Arpels of New York and dating from about 1960.

Garnet crystals have twelve or 24 faces. Those which are not red go under a variety of names, very little known except to the trade, though with the inevitable severe shortage of gemstones most in demand no doubt they will make their mark – the spessartite, almandine, andradite, demantoid, grossular, uvarovite – which, as they sound like diseases, will need considerable promotion.

The demantoid garnet is rare, green and soft, used by Victorians and first discovered in Russia in the 1860s. Grossular is also green, found in Africa and Pakistan, often speckled and similar to jade, though the trade term "Transvaal jade" fell foul of the Trade Descriptions Act in the United Kingdom. .Black garnets were widely used in mourning jewellery in the nineteenth century as an alternative to jet and other stones.

Rubellite is strictly speaking a stone called a red tourmaline, first found about 200 years ago, and was perhaps named to confuse the public with rubies. The tourmaline is a mineralogist's dream as it displays the greatest range of colours of any gem. Black tourmalines, also used for mourning jewellery, can be found in Britain on Dartmoor. Quartz is also found in Britain and indeed almost anywhere as it represents twelve per cent of all rocks on the earth. Most is unusable as gems, but some is, such as rock crystal, rarely cut as it loses its lustre, but one of the few stones which has a practical purpose. If an electric current passes through it, it pulses regularly, and a thin sliver of it is the motive power of the quartz watch and clock.

A fairly rare quartz stone is the yellow citrine, though poor-quality amethyst can be transformed into a citrine by burning it. Amethyst is among the most desirable of quartz stones, found in quantity, but only five per cent is of practical use, much of that small fragments for beads. Fine high-carat purple amethyst is therefore expensive. Cairngorm or smoky quartz was found in the Cairngorm Mountains

Above: Sapphire, diamond, ruby and gold bangles from the personal collection of Princess Salimah Aga Khan, designed in recent times by Gianmaria Buccellati.

of Scotland, and owes its popularity to the craze for all things Scottish during the early years of Queen Victoria's reign though used centuries earlier. Now comparatively rare in its natural state, the Koreans have evoked smoky quartz by processing poor amethysts. Heat treating amethysts produces green and rose quartz. Little is what it seems.

Agate may be said to be the most dramatic of gemstones, with striations, flecks of colour, wide contrasts, and, presented in slices, used on brooches, rings, almost anything. Moss agate has plant-like inclusions. Widely employed as a background in the nineteenth century, agate could be a visual disaster, as much as onyx in our own century (though the green "onyx" of Art Deco ashtrays and novelties is marble). A brown stone shot with a lively yellow is known as a tiger's eye, (a blue variant is a hawk's eye). But surely the most subtle of all the quartzes is the fleshy-reddy-brown cornelian, much used by the ancient Egyptians. There is also a dark green flecked with cornelian – the bloodstone, popular in men's signet rings, and the apple-green chrysophrase. Coming in a variety of colours, jasper was widely used by the Romans for portrait heads, mythological subjects and animals, as although hard it was carvable, and was often mottled like marble. Sardonyx is two-layered, the top one being reddish-brown, the bottom black, grey, white or brown; the Greeks and the Romans used it for

Opposite: High-fashion brooches, necklace, and ruby and diamond ring.

Left: An emerald ring, an Indian sapphire and diamond ring, a ruby and diamond bracelet, and a diamond bangle.

Above: An Art Deco aquamarine and diamond necklace.

Opposite: Prestigious ruby and diamond necklace from the French crown jewels, long in limbo.

cameos and seals, carving the top and using the bottom layer as background. Imperfections were skilfully worked into the design.

The turquoise enjoys the unenviable distinction of being the most faked and imitated stone other than the diamond. The bluest and purest turquoise is mined in Iran, and was one of the first stones valued and eagerly sought, found as it was near the surface, difficult to cut as it is fairly porous, and sometimes having an unacceptable greenish tinge, now "cured" by waxing or by doctoring it with plastic, which wears off. A heated needle will satisfy a purist but hardly a jeweler. A substance known as "Indian turquoise" enjoyed a vogue in the late 1960s, powdered turquoise bonded with plastic and set, enamel style, in a copper-rimmed container. Ridiculously cheap (less than £1 sterling) pendants and rings were wholesaled from small manufacturers in London.

The oldest turquoise mines were in Egypt, and employed at least 2000 workers, though the quality, somewhat spotty, is inferior to that of Iran. The Egyptians, to make good blue stones, used enameling techniques to simulate turquoise and were sufficiently pleased with the results to include them with the embalmed bodies of the

rulers. Turquoise was also found in America and was revered by the Native Americans who brought great skills to its processing. Large stones are often imperfect and during the eighteenth and nineteenth centuries small turquoises were set in rosettes and borders, often accompanied by pearls.

Lapis lazuli is a rich dark-blue opaque stone with brassy specks of iron pyrites, found originally only in Afghanistan, and highly valued by the ancient Egyptians. It occurs in veins in marble and is melted out by lighting fires under the marble, throwing water on the rocks which crack, releasing the lapis. Although used for rings, the best-known purpose for lapis lazuli was to be ground up and used as pigment, the blue of medieval and Renaissance paintings, enormously expensive and later replaced by commercial ultramarine but at the time possessing magical and religious overtones. Lapis lazuli was favoured by Faberge. Sodalite is one of the constituents of lapis lazuli, sometimes being mistaken for it, but the blue is often infringed by white and it is less valued. Rhodochrosite and rhodonite are popular reddish stones, attractively banded, rhodochrosite being soft, rhodonite somewhat harder, but basically run-of-the-mill stones for beads, while labradorite is a dull grey, set in cubes in silver mounts so as to catch the light and give an opal-like effect.

Better known is the delightful moonstone, blue with a soft sheen and a milky appearance, cut cabochon (round-topped) style, and appropriately there is a sunstone, yellowish red, both from Sri Lanka.

Jade is either nephrite or jadeite, the principal carving material of China, coming in all colours rather than the traditional green. Used in China from at least 3000 BC and endowed with religious and mystical properties, it was also found by Stone Age people to be ideal for tools and weapons. It is not a gemstone, and its use in the west has been self-consciously modish, and anything made in the way of jewellery compares ill with the masterpieces created in China.

Opal stands somewhat apart from the other semi-precious stones, being neither completely opaque nor transparent. Nor does it have a crystalline structure but is a hardened silica "jelly". Common opal is a dreary grey, but when shot with brilliant colours opal can be amazing; the milky appearance is due to tiny surface cracks. The rainbow-like play of colours has led to some opals being called fire opals, water opals (both from Mexico), flame opals, and harlequin opals, which is a variety showing odd patches of colour somewhat like mosaics. The rarest are the Australian black opals. Opals are fragile, mined in thin pieces, and are often mounted with some of the rock still attached. Very thin opals are "foiled" by being backed by coloured silk in a closed setting, and there are also opal doublets and triplets, often topped with rock crystal as protection.

Malachite, an attractive banded and striated green material, is a novelty material, seen at its best not in jewellery but in the malachite furniture made in Russia or inlaid into jewel and work boxes or tables. Although used in rings it is not really suitable as it is very soft (4 on the Mohs' scale).

The list of transparent stones ushered into use is endless and a complete list would read like a medical dictionary. Some are shameless substitutes for more acceptable stones, and by increasing the number

Opposite: A pair of diamond ear pendants circa 1960 designed by Van Cleef and Arpels of New York.

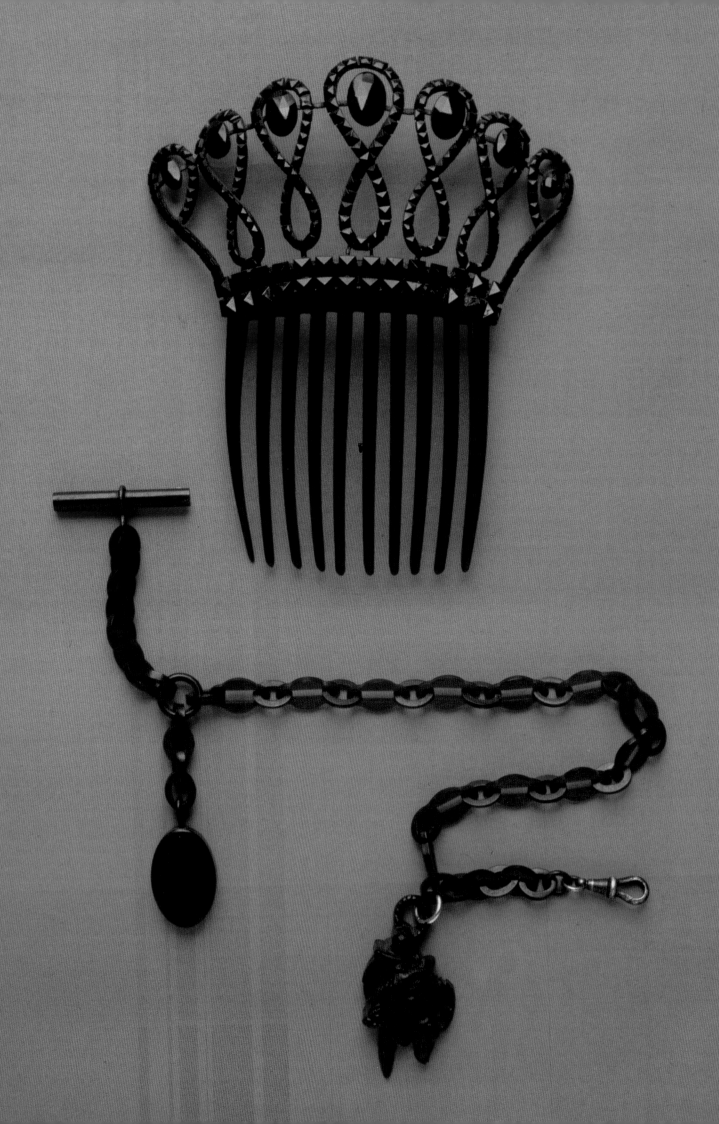

of facets great brilliance can be drawn from unpromising material. Some are capable of standing on their own such as topaz, found only in Brazil and very fragile, chrysoberyl, a yellow-green stone with a streak of light (the cat's eye) favoured by the Victorians, and the relatively obscure zoisite and tanzanite (discovered in Tanzania in 1967). Stones come and go out of fashion for no very clear reason. Opal went into decline when it was labelled an unlucky stone; amethyst fell out of view, and then reappeared. Diamonds, however, are forever.

Amber, mostly made into beads, is not a stone but fossilized resin from prehistoric conifer trees, sometimes containing tiny insects, leaf fragments or minute pieces of bark. The shores of the Baltic provided the familiar golden yellow to orange type, but the distribution is world wide and the colour range is from white to black. Large natural pieces of amber can be carved, but it can also be fused together – pressed amber. Amber is light in weight and was used to make prayer beads, enabling them to be passed easily through the fingers.

It has been endowed with all sorts of magical properties. The Etruscans were the first to appreciate it, managing to import it from the Baltic 2000 miles away though there was less desirable amber in nearby Sicily. They buried amber jewellery with their dead, the entombed insects serving as talismen. The Roman emperor Nero had an obsession with amber, supposedly because its colour matched his wife's hair. The culmination of amber craftsmanship was the Amber Room created by Frederick-William I (1688 – 1740), king of Prussia, father of Frederick the Great, who systematically mined the Baltic deposits. It disappeared in 1945.

Amber is easily imitated using copal, a resin similar to amber, glass, or plastic. When touched with a hot needle amber gives off a resinous odour and when rubbed can pick up tiny particles of paper, sometimes thought a valuable clue but not really as other materials, including some plastics, do the same. But it is a means of excluding doubtful amber which will not pick up anything.

Coral and jet are the two outsiders, lacking variation, and, although used in jewellery, have more important functions as coral was believed to have protective abilities especially for children. Consequently it was much used for teething rings and rattles (with added bells and whistles). Coral is the skeletal remains of polyp colonies, twig-like in shape, and although mostly used as they are in necklaces and bracelets a flourishing industry grew up around Naples where coral was carved into beads, cameos, and stylised centrepieces for brooches and rings.

Jet is fossilised driftwood, found in the shale beaches off Whitby in Yorkshire, England, a shiny black and made fashionable in 1861 when Queen Victoria's husband Albert died. Victoria then decreed that only black jewellery would be worn for the period of mourning, which went on for a considerable time much to the annoyance of society. The Whitby jet industry went into overdrive, though there was competition from black glass ("French jet") and although after 20 years the mourning period lapsed jet continued to be spasmodically used in jewellery, though it can never be other than a novelty material.

Opposite: Whitby jet watch chain and hair comb of about 1870 at the very limits of jewellery.

ADORNMENT AND PRESTIGE

The use of jewellery as personal adornment is closely bound up with the kind of costume in fashion. Where costume was opulent, accompanying jewellery was obliged to compete with it and the result could be horrendous. Horace Walpole (1717 – 1797), author, anecdotalist and wit, reviewed the many portraits of Queen Elizabeth I:

> Elizabeth appears like an Indian idol, totally composed of pearls and necklaces. A pale Roman nose, a head of hair loaded with crowns and powdered with diamonds, a vast ruff, a vaster farthingale, and a bushel of pearls are features by which everyone knows at once the picture of Elizabeth.

Although certain types of jewellery, such as the locket, fall in and out of fashion, most were known in the ancient world and have continued to be worn. Toe-rings may have enjoyed a brief period of popularity, but bracelets, necklaces, necklets (lightweight necklaces), diadems (tiaras), fibulae (brooches with a safety-pin type fitting), have rarely gone out of fashion for any length of time, though equipped with more sophisticated and safer fastenings.

There are items that have become obsolete, such as the ferroniere, a small jewel hanging by a narrow ribbon and so arranged that the ornament falls in the middle of the forehead. It was first worn in Renaissance times and in vogue during the early nineteenth century, featuring in portraits of the period. A jewel was often replaced by a locket, and the ribbon was often black or substituted by a fine chain.

Throughout much of the last 1000 years gold chains have been worn, often heavy, frequently of great intricacy, the last flowering

Above: Japanese jewellery is little known, but to judge by this charming hair comb of painted brass of the nineteenth century it should be, though it might be stretching a point to define painted brass as jewellery.

Opposite: Eagle clasp which belonged to Gisela (c. 990–1043), wife of the German Emperor Conrad II. It is beautifully crafted in gold, enamel and gemstones.

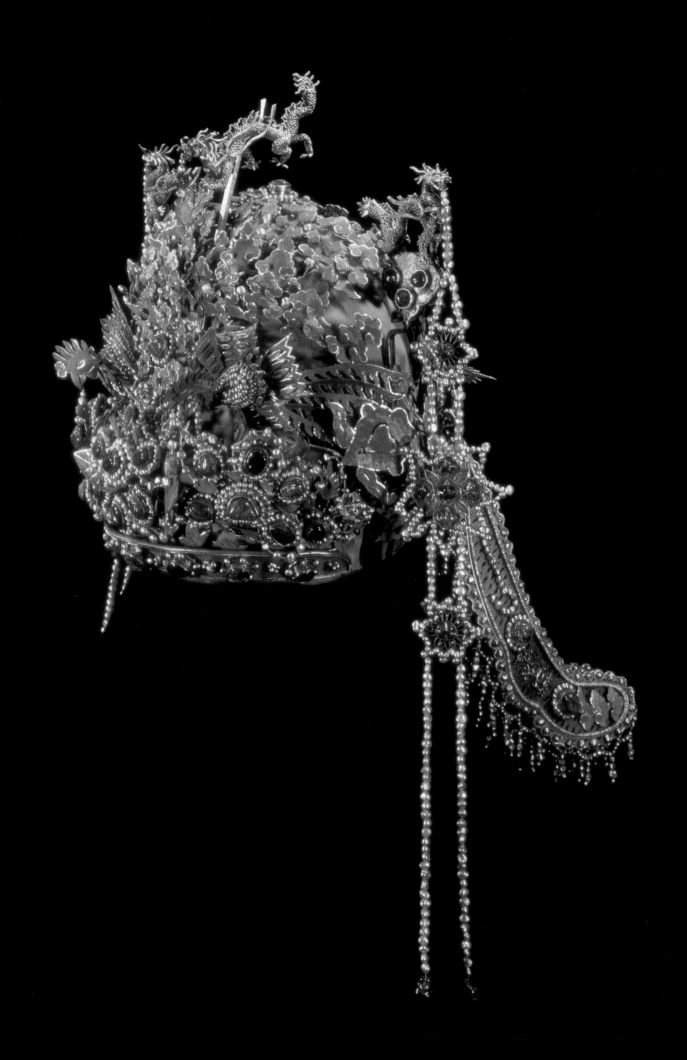

amongst men being the Albert watch chain worn across the waistcoat. The watch was tucked into the waistcoat pocket. The Albert was also used to carry seals and similar articles, and was worn not only by the middle classes but the "improved" working classes. For foremen and supervisors they were a token of superiority, even if they were only made of brass and not gold. There was in the nineteenth century a kind of equivalent for women, the chatelaine, a chain worn around the waist from which was suspended keys and other objects, often worn by the upper domestics such as housekeepers.

With the rise of the feudal system, there were great class divisions, expressed in dress and jewellery. During certain periods the peasantry were forced to wear certain colours to differentiate them from their betters. There were stern laws in medieval and even Tudor times that restricted the wearing of jewellery to the nobility and royalty. There was thus no input from the growing middle-classes, so important in later years in furniture, silver and ceramics. Nor was there a peasant jewellery in Britain. Proscriptions against lesser folk wearing jewellery was not restricted to the west; they operated also in India and the east.

It was not only necessary to establish one's class by what one wore with what accessories, but to try and overwhelm one's equals by a peacock display. Only with women, and then only during certain periods, was there any refinement in the jewellery they wore, often in the

Above: The signet ring of King Louis IX of France (1215 - 70) of gold and enamel.

Opposite: The Phoenix Coronet, an empress's hair piece from the Ding tomb in Beijing dating from the Ming dynasty (1268 - 1644) and of great style and bravura.

Overleaf: Spanish stomacher, a word with many meanings including a man's waistcoat, but this time a chest adornment, eighteenth century in gold set with rose-cut diamonds.

Above: A magnificent swan pendant of about 1590 in gold, enamel, pearl and gemstones, possibly from the Netherlands.

Opposite: Clasp bearing the fleur-de-lis, the royal arms of France, said to have belonged to King Louis IX (1215 - 70), of gold and gemstones.

form of a gold necklace and little other adornment, though there were curiosities when fashion decreed that men and women should be hung with bells.

During the Renaissance, brocades, velvets, satins and silks became increasingly used, heavy clothing which needed heavy jewellery, such as substantial gold chains, to complement it. Earlier eccentricities were discarded – the shoes often three feet long, and the fantastic pointed hats; it was decreed that the woman's form was not ideally S-shaped with the stomach protruding. Great attention was paid to women's hair, the rich braiding pearls into their hair and crowning their heads with elaborate diadems encrusted with jewels. Women were preoccupied with their appearance, bleaching and dyeing their hair blonde, and painting their faces, neck, breasts, eyes and lips, a practice often prohibited and equally often ignored. The face was adorned with beauty patches, and the pupils of the eyes were enlarged using belladonna. The extent of these practices varied throughout Europe, with Italy and later France the leaders of fashion.

The results of these cosmetic efforts are rarely evident in the pictures of the period from which we can ascertain a good deal, certainly the kind of jewellery that was worn by both men and women. Men's outdoor cloaks were often pinned with an elaborate brooch. Women's necklaces, which began as men's wear, were often extremely elaborate, in a woven band, or in three sections connected by gemstones. Sometimes several very substantial necklaces were worn together. This reached a summit in the late Victorian and Edwardian periods when a "choker" necklace of pearls could consist of ten separate strands. When a woman wore a cloak about the shoulders, they were often kept together by a gold chain with elaborate roseate brooches at each end.

At certain periods a high forehead was considered beautiful, and

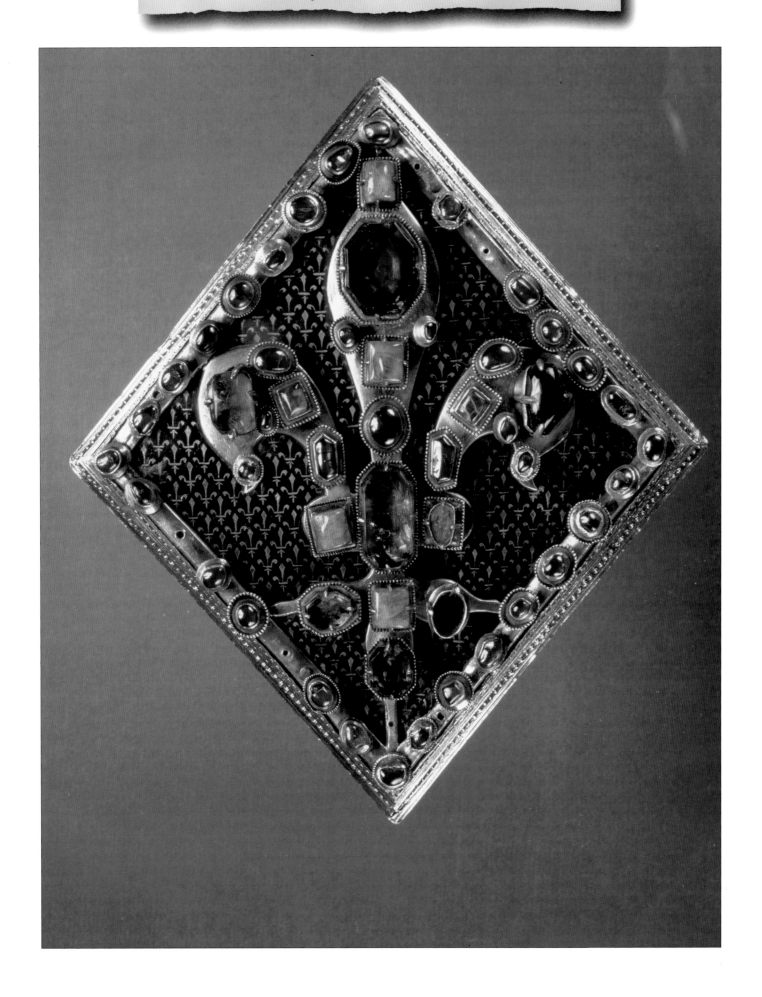

Above: Bangle set with portrait miniature of Charlotte, Duchess of Northumberland.

the hair was shaved. The hair was combed straight back, held in place by a band and an imposing brooch of some prominence, pointed upwards, a curious eccentricity and one would have thought not wholly free from danger.

The most important piece of jewellery is the ring, especially among men for whom in modern times it became often the only piece of everyday jewellery. It has the advantage that it has to be comfortable (to a degree) and cannot be piled high with extravagances. There was a ring for all purposes: the decade ring, dating from the fourteenth century, took the place of a rosary, with ten projections, each representing an Ave and a larger protrusion, the Paternoster. The eternity ring is fairly modern, usually of platinum, the gems traditionally diamonds, rubies or sapphires, often set alternately. The gimmal ring is a betrothal ring, a combination of two rings so formed that they only form a perfect ring when worn together. An engaged couple would keep one incomplete ring each until the marriage. Jewish ceremonial rings are kept in the synagogue and reserved for marriage ceremonies, and bear a representation of a structure believed to be the Ark of the Covenant. Examples exist from the sixteenth and seventeenth centuries. The keeper ring, now obsolete, was a heavy gold ring heavily

Above: The so-called Phoenix Jewel bearing a portrait of Elizabeth I in a setting with floral motifs.

engraved or chased, and supposed to be worn with the wedding ring as a safeguard against the accidental loss of the wedding ring, though one would have thought that it was as easy to lose two rings as one.

The marquise ring was popular in the latter part of the eighteenth century, boat or oval shaped and filling the space between the knuckle and the first joint. Very elaborate, they often consisted of a diamond or diamond group on enamel or glass on gold , with the diamonds, often grouped into a pattern, sometimes set in silver. Their purpose as in much historical jewellery is obscure, and were obviously tokens of prestige. Moss agate was sometimes used instead of enamel or glass as the base. The materna ring was invented to celebrate motherhood (sapphire for a girl, ruby for a boy) but it did not prove popular. It was thought up by the jewellery trade to increase custom, as was true of the eternity ring which has no basis except to encourage married bliss.

The posy ring, sometimes known as the motto or chanson. ring, carries an engraved message on the outside or inside; the posy comes from "poesy" (verse), though confusingly old posy rings were decorated with flowers. The poison ring had a hidden hinged compartment, but mementos, religious items and possibly cosmetics were as often contained as poison. A more venomous poison ring had a spike, though it

Left: A diamond ring by the jeweller Chaumet, an Edwardian diamond collar, and a diamond diadem.

is difficult to see how this could be worn safely in polite society.

Seals were used on rings, and also mounted in gold and worn round the neck, or suspended from a chain. .They were carved in all materials. The Romans and Greeks used scenes from mythology, selecting the stone to suit the subject. The signet ring is also of great antiquity, worn as a symbol of authority and as proof of identity to banks and similar institutions, and usually featured initials, coats of arms, or symbols of the owner.

It was not until the sixteenth century that the wedding ring had an official role in the marriage ceremony. It was originally highly decorated and not at all plain. From 1576 – 1798 only the highest carat gold (22 carat) was used, but after then 18 carat became the norm except from 1942 during World War II when in the United Kingdom 9-carat rings were decreed. To some extent, platinum has replaced gold in wedding rings.

After the Renaissance, when there was style, discretion, and a degree of appropriateness in jewellery, and there were goldsmiths of genius such as Benvenuto Cellini (1500 – 1571), jewellery seems to have changed its role and pursued its own path, wearers and makers seeming intent on flaunting their acquisitions and disdaining taste and decorum. Much middle-range jewellery of the Renaissance has not survived as pieces were recycled.

With new methods of cutting, all stones could be brought to a pitch of brilliance, and there seemed a desire to see how many diverse and ill-assorted stones could be massed together with opulent gold surrounds. Arthur Hamilton Smith writing in the eleventh edition of the Encyclopaedia Britannica summed up the post-Elizabethan scene:

> During the seventeenth and eighteenth centuries we see only a mechanical kind of excellence, the results of the mere tradition of the workshop – the lingering of the power which when wisely directed had done so much and so well, but now simply living on traditional forms, often combined in the most incongruous fashion.

Opposite: A Spanish diamond, gold, and enamel pendant formed as an eagle from about 1620.

Below: Jewellery in the form of tiger heads.

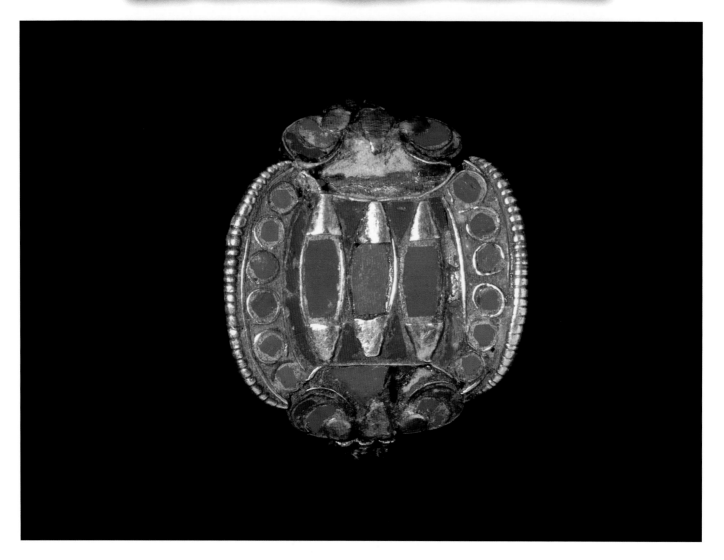

Above: Electrum is natural gold with between 20% and 50% silver content. This inlaid Egyptain ring is from between 1550 and 1307 BC.

Opposite: Georgian jewellery is not particularly noteworthy, but this George IV gold and amethyst parture (necklace, bracelets, earrings and brooch) is exceptional. It dates from about 1830.

Jewellery of the eighteenth century is curiously anonymous and tame, and although there is no question that techniques were supreme, that imitation stones were being perfected (opaline was at its best 1780 – 1800), there seemed to be an inability to be at all adventurous. Factory-made jewellery made its appearance.

One of the reasons for the lack of distinction of eighteenth-century jewellery was that it was necessarily subordinated to the extravagances of passing fashions, such as the hair styles of women. When Louis XVI came to the throne in 1774 ladies' coiffures had become so enormous that the mouth was at a point almost halfway between the top of the hair and the soles of the feet. The hair was upswept and supplemented by pads of horsehair. Even the simplest of hair styles gave shelter to vermin. Although jewellery was used to adorn the head, it was completely overwhelmed by the coiffure itself. Jewellery did not seem to have a major role. Which is surprising as the eighteenth century saw the increasing power and influence of women in everyday life.

England was to some extent spared the excesses of the French. The costume of the middle classes was becoming plainer and more functional and was having an effect on the upper classes. In 1739 individual groups of young people in London imitated servants' garb in order

to seem modern. The hooped skirt of the last quarter of the eighteenth century was also not conductive to the display of jewellery.

Much of the evidence comes from portraiture as the jewellery itself, unless of stunning quality, was still often recycled. A portrait of Marie Antoinette by Janinet depicts the hair laden with pearls, ribbons and feathers, but otherwise little jewellery is worn, not even a necklace. The only body jewellery worn in Thomas Gainsborough's full-length portrait of Queen Charlotte is a small circular brooch on the V-shaped neckline. Jewellery also competed for attention with accessories such as fans.

There was a divergence between the jewellery worn by the middle classes and that worn by royalty and the upper classes, and there was also competition between the somewhat affected simplicity of women, mostly young and impressionable, who were in thrall to the romantic movement and the old order. There was a fashion for women's clothes in the Greek style, suitably amended for modern life, and such a life style decreed that jewellery should be restrained, if worn at all.

The waist had moved from below the breasts to its natural level, accepted by all and dress styles amongst both men and women became extravagant. Napoleon had given permission for his military officers to design their own uniforms, with gold braid and extravagant trimmings, and their wives were encouraged to dress up to their husbands with ever more varied outfits. If Napoleon saw a woman wearing the same outfit twice he was very displeased and few crossed Napoleon when he was out of humour.

English tailoring for men was now reckoned to be the best in the world and refinement of men's clothing, apart from the wear of the dandies, resulted in less excess and a minimum of jewellery. The most important

Below: Known as the Mancini Pearls, these lavish earrings were given by Louis XIV the Sun King to Maria Mancini in the seventeenth century.

Above: King Louis XIV (1638 - 1715) period jewellery, a sapphire and enamelled gold ring, and an emerald and enamelled gold ring.

aspect of men's clothing was concentrated around the neck. The collars of shirt and coat, together with the cravat, were intricately arranged, and could take hours to perfect. The cravat and its successors were to produce an entirely individual range of men's jewellery, most notably the stock-pin used by the hunting fraternity and the tie-pin, first termed a stick pin, which were often topped by precious stones which were equally often taken from the pins and inserted into rings. The pins were sometimes made from gold or silver and fully hall marked, and the heads could be cameos, miniatures featuring pets or people, or carved crystals. Tie-pins were sufficiently valued to warrant designs by Peter Carl Faberge. The tie-pin was, in the twentieth century, sometimes, not excepting rings, the only article of jewellery worn by the man in the street.

After the fall of Napoleon, men's fashions in France followed those of Britain, while women's fashions followed France, often to an extent bordering on the obsessive. During the nineteenth century gemstones were more common and cheaper, especially in Britain for which the Empire provided its treasures. New technologies enabled systematic mining to be carried out on a large scale. Jewellery was often worn massed, especially by the women of the rising middle classes anxious to assert their authority and their immense wealth.

The kind of jewellery was always influenced by the costume of the

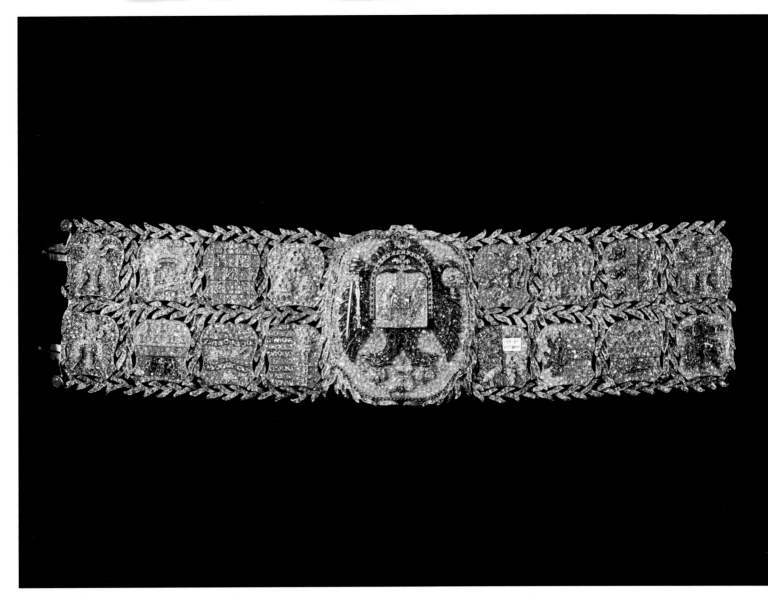

period, by the availability of gemstones and their cost, and by the social climate. When the society is in a state of flux as it was in the last half of the nineteenth century, the types of jewellery echoed this. It is high time to demolish the myth of Victoriana, a blanket term to cover the quaint, the outrageous, and the essence of bad taste. What is commonly thought of as the Victorian period lasted no more than two or three decades, the 1850s and the 1860s, subtly changing in the 1870s with the introduction of ideas and a way of looking at things which even today is thoroughly modern.

There is no surer indication of this than in Victorian jewellery. There were the ponderous parures, a set of jewellery which could be customized for the occasion, and there was the restrained jewellery of the upper classes. Jewellery was realistic and revivalist, and also responded to the wave of fads characteristic of a culture in danger of losing its way. Extensive archaeological discoveries in Egypt resulted in an enthusiasm for snake bracelets, necklaces, and rings. Flowers on a brooch were as much like flowers as it was possible to make them, and realism was highly valued. Some were made *tremblant* so that

Above: A gold and jewelled presentation armorial bracelet associated with the Austrian court, probably German c. 1845 - 55.

Opposite: Indian jewellery is inclined to be overpowering. Size and intricacy were more important than quality, though the skills of the jewellers were unsurpassed by those in the west. The seven-jewel necklace represents on each enamelled-gold jewel a planet within the Indian solar system. The connected beads are of emerald. The necklace is set with colourless gems. The bangle is of enamel and diamonds.

Left: Fine jewellery in glass, diamond and gold by Réné Lalique (1860 - 1945). The dividing line between fine gemstones and natural substances of no value was starting to be crossed.

Above: A diamond and ruby heart-shaped brooch.

they moved. Realism was very evident in novelty jewellery, such as silver insects, which, however, indicate a change of emphasis, a willingness to deviate from convention, a portent of the future. There was also the influence of foreign cultures, especially that of Japan.

The most popular brooch was probably the flower made from diamonds, sometimes with added pearls and moonstones, with tiny coloured gems introduced for fine detail. The Victorians were passionate about gardening and flowers. Many plants were introduced to Europe early in the century, including the tiger lily, the wisteria, the chrysanthemum, and many types of roses. The fuschia had been discovered in the eighteenth century but was not valued until after 1830. What is thought of as the quintessential Victorian pot plant, the aspidistra, was first known in 1822. Flowers also carried subtle messages; in 1856 a dictionary of 700 flowers was published with their meanings. Such brooches served as love tokens. Great expertise was used to emulate flowers by jewelers, but they did not serve as sources of inspiration until the art nouveau period, where flowers such as the iris and the lily were presented in a formalised form in jewellery, glass, ceramics and as adornments to furniture.

In the 1860s and 1870s earrings, both large and small, became fashionable, sometimes made in jet, tortoiseshell, coral and ivory. These depicted flowers as well as more unusual subjects such as pea-pods, ears of corns, and bunches of grapes using seed pearls. Towards the end of the 1860s there was a fashion for necklaces composed of gold leaves and foliage, usually with detachable pendants which could be worn as brooches. Throughout the period lockets were popular, containing miniatures, photographs, or locks of hair, and these were often lavishly ornamented with diamonds and precious stones or intricately engraved with flowers or foliage. Towards the end of the century there was a vogue for celestial jewellery featuring crescent moons and stars in diamonds or pearls, especially popular as hair ornaments on pins or combs, and the gradual involvement of women in sport resulted in sporting brooches depicting fox masks, hounds, horses, riding whips, bicycles, tennis rackets and indeed almost anything. The diamond horseshoe was especially popular.

High-quality gem stones were available to all but the working classes as many of the stones were mined in the British Empire and those that were not came from parts of the world, such as South America, where Britain played a major role.

Below: A Renaissance pendant with a feline theme, very realistic.

When gemstones such as emeralds and sapphires were readily available to the jewellery-wearing classes there was no enormous kudos to be obtained from wearing them, and there was just as much interest in wearing jewellery made from fossils, bog oak, and other natural objects and materials. They could be seen to be at least what they purported to be, but with the gemstones there was no way of telling, without a detailed examination by an expert, whether they were genuine or imitations. And apart from gemstones and curiosities a totally new kind of jewellery was being made. From iron and steel.

Except under controlled conditions few women wear their best jewellery in everyday life, and fear of theft or mugging is as good a reason as any for women to wear imitations or jewellery made from materials inherently valueless, such as iron and steel, and, in the present century, aluminium.

During the Napoleonic Wars Prussian women, in order to help their country, gave up their diamonds and gold to be sold for the state, and wore black iron jewellery, the business starting in Silesia in the eighteenth century but transferring to Berlin in 1804, giving us its name – Berlin iron jewellery. It was usually moulded, and was matt black, but some pieces were later lac-

Above: A Victorian diamond tiara of about 1870 in a fitted Garrard case. Garrard were the royal jewellers.

Opposite: A highly intricate pendant commemorating the Battle of Naseby in 1645 during the English Civil War, an unusual theme, and one wonders who, if anyone, would have worn it. Certainly not Oliver Cromwell, who won the battle.

quered or enamelled, and after the war it became so fashionable that items were framed in gold. It was popular until at least the middle of the nineteenth century, and some pieces bore inscriptions and dates such as *Gold gab ich fur Eisen 1813* ("I gave gold for iron 1813"). Necklaces and bracelets formed a large part of the output, sometimes combined with cameos and mythological figures, often cunningly constructed of wire of a spider's-web delicacy. Iron jewellery was also made in France, and in Britain, some designed by Augustus Pugin (1812 – 1852), chunky and Gothic. Pugin was the leading figure of the Victorian Gothic Revival.

Cut-steel and marcasite jewellery are far more common and popular. These are often confused. Marcasite is made up of small particles of iron pyrites set in silver claws or pans in the same way as gemstones are set. Cut steel, which shares the same designs, is made of small faceted heads of steel often riveted to a thin back plate or in the form of chains, used for watches, necklaces and chatelaines. Cut-steel work was referred to as early as 1598 in England, with Woodstock in Oxfordshire as the centre. There is doubt about what this cut-steel adventure was, though the raw material was old horseshoe nails. As

early as 1762 cut-steel jewellery was taken up commercially by the first modern industrial manufacturer, Matthew Boulton, at his factory in Soho, Birmingham, though buttons and buckles formed the bulk of his output. The buttons and buckles are a good deal more interesting than the fine jewellery of the time. Some of his jewellery and art objects incorporated jasper-ware plaques by Wedgwood, though references to jewellery are rare before the nineteenth century. At the coronation of Napoleon the ladies of the court wore tiaras of cut steel incorporating motifs such as the eagle with outswept wings.

The wearing of cut-steel jewellery became moderately fashionable as women were increasingly becoming more assertive and individualistic, throwing off the shackles of tradition and deciding for themselves what they would wear in the way of adornment. They were less interested in being walking symbols of status. Metal jewellery became illustrative of the modern age and modern interests, featuring locomotives and all subjects previously depicted in diamonds, gems, gold and silver and was available at a fraction of the cost. It was often stamped out from thin steel plate for the mass market.

All kinds of materials were pressed into the service of new dress accessories such as the hat pin, including cloth, feathers, and real insects. Lalique himself was not too proud to design hat pins. A factor of late-nineteenth-century jewellery was the extensive import and export from and to newly industrialised countries such as Bohemia (later part of Czechoslovakia). The proliferation of ideas led to innovation and invention, with nation vying with nation to create ever more novel pieces, a trend which reached its peak in the mid-1890s and the arrival of art nouveau, which upstaged everything that had gone before.

Opposite: Two Renaissance pendant jewels.

Below: Silver chatelaine, with the maker's mark W.N., assay mark Chester 1902. The chatelaine was a chain worn round the waist to which keys, scissors, and other useful items were suspended, worn by the lady of the house or more often the housekeeper.

ART NOUVEAU

The greatest period in English, European and American jewellery was during the art nouveau years, which were at their peak between 1895 and 1910. The entire tradition of jewellery was jettisoned. The Paris jeweler Leon Rouvenat had provided his workmen with a fresh bunch of lilacs every day for them to copy during the High Victorian period. The results were stilted and lifeless, mere mechanical copying, a characteristic of much Victorian high art. The art nouveau jewelers sought their floral inspiration elsewhere, though sometimes relying on pattern books such as Alphonse Mucha's *Documents decoratifs* of 1902. As with the Victorian jewelers, flowers and plants were key elements in their repertory, but they formalised and distorted them, finding them ideal for one of the basic features of art nouveau design, not only in jewellery – the sinuous and serpentine curve.

Art nouveau did not appear from nowhere. It had its roots in the Arts and Crafts Movement of the 1880s, which rejected the machine age which was thought debilitating and a threat to civilization. The jewellery of the Arts and Crafts Movement is amateurish and inclined to be dull as the practitioners were general purpose do-it-yourself enthusiasts without jewel-making experience. The calm stillness and economy of Japanese art was another influence and many thought that the relationship between nature and design evident in Japanese art had been lost in Europe, some declared since the Middle Ages. But perhaps the most important was the appearance of scores of talented designers who pursued their own way, regardless of commercial considerations, though it says much for the intelligence and taste

Above: A traditional diamond and enamel pendant of the art nouveau period; not everything was adventurous and novel.

Opposite: A Lalique piece of about 1900, opalescent enamel in a silver frame of tangled hair crowned with four large poppies.

Above: Arts and Crafts jewellery designed for Liberty's by Archibald Knox (1864 - 1933), a waist clasp 1904, pendant and chain set, and a further waist clasp with repoussé (raised in relief) design. Knox was one of the most important figures bridging the Arts and Crafts/ art nouveau styles.

Opposite: British art nouveau was less extravagant than the French, though no less significant. These three pieces are a Medusa-head brooch in yellow metal, ivory and enamel, designed by George Hunt, a Liberty silver buckle bearing the Liberty trade mark "Cymric", and a white metal necklace designed by Arthur and Georgina Gaskin.

of the public that many designers were feted and proved that there was a demand for the new and unconventional, even the outright bizarre. Many of these artists, such as Christopher Dresser (1834 – 1904) and Charles Rennie Mackintosh (1868 – 1928) operated in many areas of the applied arts, and there was constant interaction . Jewellery designs could appear, suitably amended, in furniture motifs, glass, and ceramics, and vice versa.

There is no one single essence of art nouveau. It can be seen as a blanket term to describe the intense wave of experimentation flooding through Europe and America. It could be geometric, even brutalist, as in some of the work of Dresser, or it could be lushly opulent such as much French art nouveau, also described as having a debauched sensuality. Art nouveau jewellery tended towards the latter, representing wriggling marine plants, writhing abstract forms resembling tentacles, rippling hair, the female form, and "whiplash" motifs. In Britain the only earlier jewellery even remotely resembling it was that made by the ancient Celts. The jewellery, especially the key piece, the brooch, could be simple or it could be enormously complex, using gold, silver, gemstones, enamels, glass, horn, mother of pearl, and steel, just in one piece. It could be overpowering or it could be quietly restrained. But above all there was endless invention and innovation.

Above: A coiled snake pendant with chain in gold, enamel and pearls, by Lalique, c.1900.

There were favourite subjects to which the jewelers returned time and time again, such as fantasy insects, particularly the dragonfly and the butterfly. This in itself was not new. In the 1870s there had been a plague of naturalistic insects descending on the veils, hats, and jacket fronts of the fashionable so much so that Mary Haweis in her *The Art of Beauty* of 1878 fumed against the presence of such creatures where they would not be allowed to be if alive – and if alive would have scared the wearers half to death, especially if the insects were snails, slugs and spiders. The markings and veining of butterfly and dragonfly wings were a challenge to the jewelers, who set out to present them often translucently and even created the wings so that they moved. Jewellers responded to any challenge, as Galle did in glass. If it was difficult so much the better. Never in the arts has there been so much joy in creation. The spider with its web was typical of the challenges offered.

Entwined writhing serpents, a traditional theme dating back to the Egyptians, was another constant motif, much used by Lalique, best known for his glass. The frog and the lizard make their appearance, as well as the chameleon, the shifting colours presenting a considerable problem to even the deftest designer. Most birds were depicted especially the peacock and the swan, though owls, vultures, flights of sparrows, and eagles were also used. These had to a lesser degree been used before, but there was one subject that was wholly new – the naked female form , often subtly erotic, and the female face, occasionally bewilderingly realistic, even ugly. The face was often only an excuse for the jeweller to render the hair; the flowing tresses of the art nouveau woman lent themselves to endless invention, though curiously enough it was not a very popular trend in real life. Though real life had nothing to do with the style. Those who practised art nouveau lived in a fantasy world, as did many of those who bought it, and it is not surprising that there was a great outcry amongst the traditionalists against everything art nouveau represented – decadence, the fin de siecle, escapism, art for art's sake. Had the opportunity arose, many would have prosecuted it, as they did a prime representative of the

Below: The hair comb was an essential art nouveau dress accessory, and this characteristic example made by Fred Partridge was made from enamel, moonstone, and horn, long obsolete and newly rediscovered by designers.

genre, Oscar Wilde, in 1895. Art nouveau was the Internet of the 1890s, 1900s and 1910s , impossible to regulate.

It also parallels an interesting social trend – the emancipation of women and their changing roles in society. Art nouveau jewellery was feminine and capricious, and was no longer worn to announce the status of a husband. Power jewellery was consigned to history, and except among a few coteries would never emerge again. The depiction of women on jewellery, naked or otherwise, was not always accepted. Although a French jeweller had designed a bracelet in 1841 showing two half-naked women in a saucy posture, it was held by many that the "aesthetic design rules" do not allow a woman to wear on her head, around her neck, or on her breast the image of a human figure. Sometimes the naked woman was metamorphosed into a mermaid or a fairy, as had been extensively done in paintings to avert criticism by the over-puritanical.

Crucial to the impact of art nouveau jewellery was a searching look at the technologies available. This had

happened in glass and furniture, where techniques from prehistory had been overturned in a few years. In the applied arts there was a desire to make the material, whatever it was, seem organic, so much so that it was often difficult to see what the material was. This could result in weird oddities, such as much French art nouveau furniture where the structure of wood seems to have been re-created atom by atom to be something else, or masterpieces such as the glassware of Galle. In jewellery "hard" metals and gems were transformed, so that the materials seemed to be melting into each other. Some gems were more suitable than others. Diamonds were used, often as "edging", but they were not amenable to the revitalising treatment, by their very nature demanding separate attention. Opal was a favourite gem, and horn was one of the materials, scorned for centuries, which was re-evaluated for its versatility. Hard and brittle, horn is not the ideal material for jewellery, but many jewellers treated it, the recipe for which has been lost. Glass was also used, often ground down and refired to give a gem-like appearance. Moonstone was popular as was chalcedony. No gem was picked for its expense or desirability, only for its place in the grand pattern.

Much used was enamel, glass in powder form fused to a metal surface under heat. Two of the main forms are *cloisonne*, in which the enamel fills little metal pockets or cells of metal, and *plique a jour*,

Above: The dragonfly was a favourite art nouveau motif, especially amongst jewellers who fancied the challenge of the wings. This fine specimen is in gold, diamonds, and enamel.

Opposite: Modest jewellery of the Arts and Crafts type, well crafted but lacking real individuality.

Previous pages: A selection of typical Arts and Crafts and art nouveau brooches including designs by Charles Horner, Murrle Bennett, and William H. Haseler, all towards the end of the period when some of the impetus and enthusiasm was going.

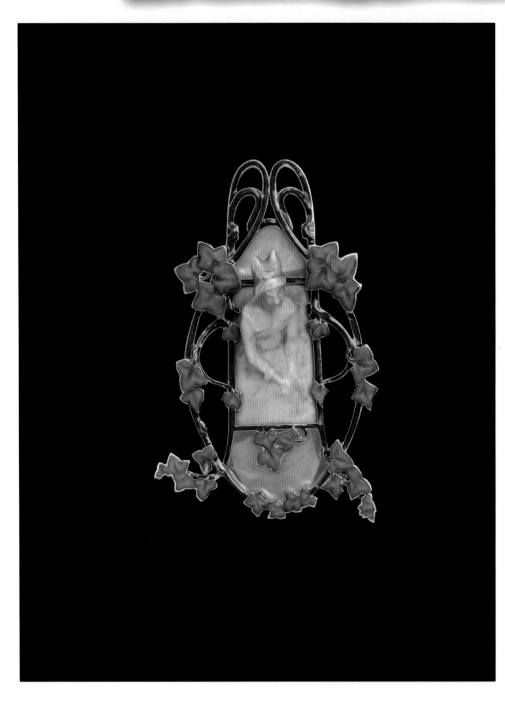

Above: Entitled "Bretonniere", a Lalique gold, horn, and enamel pendant of the turn of the century.

Opposite: A strongly individualistic pendant by Henry Wilson (1864 - 1934). Wilson designed a great deal of metalwork, which seems to have influenced this piece. His jewellery has been characterised as lumpy.

which art nouveau rediscovered and which gives the effect of a stained glass window. The enamelling is carried out in the same way, but the metal base is removed by acid or the enamel does not cling to it as in *cloisonne*. Although very fragile, it was ideal for transparent and semi-transparent effects, as in butterfly wings, but it could hardly be used for brooches or anything pinned to fabrics as the translucency would be lost. Jewellery using *pique a jour* was therefore non-utilitarian, show pieces for display rather than mundane wear. Much of this is true of a good deal of the jewellery of the time, too delicate for everyday life and essentially art objects to be admired.

The other type of enamelling process greatly liked by the turn of the century jewellers was *champleve* with the metal background hollowed out and then filled, ideal for work on a larger scale and a feature of furniture decoration. This was much easier to do and less intricate than the other types of enamelling. It can thus be carried out with less expertise, and it is not surprising that it was a popular technique for those manufacturing jewellers looking towards a mass market for art nouveau, a market which never fully materialised. Art nouveau lasted until the outbreak of World War I, and had it not been interrupted its impact would have been more significant on the general public. It was a truly civilized art movement which ended when a type of civilization ended. When the lights went out of Europe, as Lord Grey put it, the lights also went out of the applied arts and were never to fully recover, even after 80 years. Many of the art nouveau devices were picked up again in the 1920s and 1930s, but they were used, often without conviction, as decorative touches.

Although the most ravishing and spectacular pieces were made in France, the English scene was far from dead, the enthusiasm for art nouveau fostered by the most influential retail outlet of the time,

Above: An art nouveau head framed by butterfly wings, a successful if outlandish design. The materials include soapstone, little used in the west in any form of fine art and normally disregarded as fit for nothing else but novelty items. In the east it was a viable cut-price substitute for jade.

Liberty's of Regent Street, founded by Sir Arthur Liberty (1843 – 1917) in 1875, initially specializing in Japonaiserie and the Oriental but branching out to take in all the most progressive applied arts including silver, jewellery, pewter, and furniture. Liberty opened a branch in Paris in 1890. His counterpart in France was Samuel Bing (1838 – 1919) who opened his shop L'Art Nouveau in 1895 and gave the unformalised style a name. One of Liberty's designers was C. R. Ashbee (1863 – 1942), a leading figure in the Arts and Crafts Movement, founder in 1888 of the Guild and School of Handicraft in the East End of London, the pupils of which were to carry on his message stressing the superiority, moral and artistic, of hand-made work, a message he was to discard in 1910 when he reluctantly accepted that the machine age had arrived. He exhibited widely throughout Europe, and was a powerful force in consolidating art nouveau in America . He was one of the first Europeans to admire and praise the work of Frank Lloyd Wright. Ashbee's jewellery was in a low-key French style, a favourite motif being the peacock, wrought in silver, gold and pearls.

Respectability was given to the movement by the magazine *The Studio*, started in 1893, which from the start supported progressive artistic movements, ran competitions, and publicised Liberty's. There had been magazines associated with avant garde movements, but they

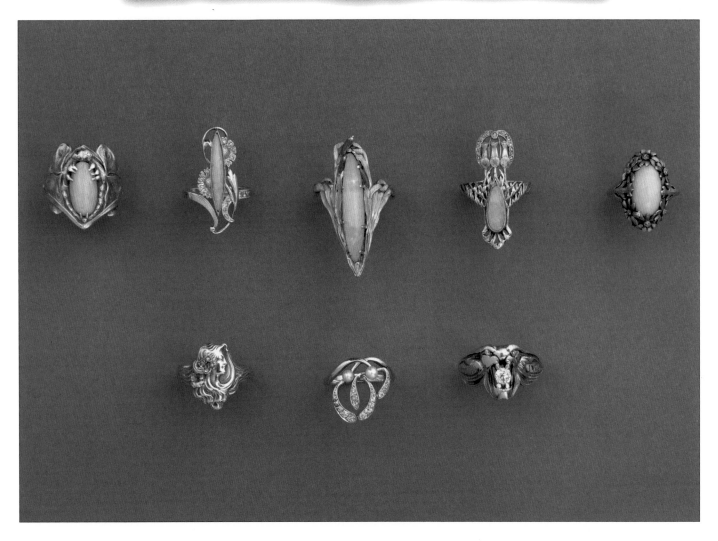

Above: A selection of French art nouveau rings. The ring was not really suitable for the art nouveau jeweller's art as because of its function little could be done to drastically revitalise the form.

had been low circulation hobby-type journals, and the importance of *The Studio* was considerable as it was bought by the young and forward looking, the perfect market for the new designs. The redoubtable *Magazine of Art* also ventured into the new waters with a series of articles called *What is Art Nouveau?* and invited readers' reactions, which by and large were hostile, even venomous.

The proliferation of exhibitions throughout the last half of the nineteenth century, beginning in London with the Great Exhibition of 1851, encouraged a generally accepted European style, which was revivalist and eclectic Art nouveau broke the mould for although there were common elements each nation took a different direction. There were important exhibitions in Liege in 1895, Venice in 1899, Vienna in 1900, and Turin in 1902, and the practitioners vied with each other in outrage and invention. The most powerful and aggressive art nouveau came from Germany and Scandinavia, known as *Jugendstil*, from the forward-looking magazine *Jugend*. Italian art nouveau was inclined to be tame, and was known in the country as the *stile Liberty*.

Liberty was so impressed by German art nouveau that in 1897 he imported *Jugendstil* metalware, and created his own. Liberty jewellery was marketed under the name Cymric.

Liberty also advanced the Celtic revival, using the skills of Archibald Knox (1864 – 1933), and it was Knox who inaugurated the

Overleaf: A display of late art nouveau jewellery (1908 - 1915), some designed by Charles Horner.

Cymric range. Knox was born in the Isle of Man and had been a keen student of Celtic work. All the jewellery was hand made, but given a svelte machine-finished appearance. It was made in silver and gold, often set with turquoise or mother of pearl or enamelled, and a characteristic feature was the amusing use of ill-shaped pearl drops.

Many famous artists designed art nouveau jewellery including the corruscating Glasgow School artist Jessie M. King, only recently being evaluated as a major artist, Edward Burne-Jones, famous for his androgynous nudes, and the fin de siecle illustatrator Charles Ricketts. Other talented designers are known mainly by their work for Liberty, such as Oliver Baker (1859 – 1938), who specialized in belt buckles but also did jewellery. They all regarded art nouveau jewellery as a major art form, a view that had not been in evidence since the Renaissance in Italy, and that is the way that it should be regarded today, not a costume accesssory.

In the United States, art nouveau jewellery followed the same path as in Britain. Until the 1880s jewellery was conventional, often imported from London and Birmingham, with cameos, exceptionally popular in America, from Italy. In 1850 the government imposed duty on imported jewellery, encouraging a home industry. As the Americans had been the first to open up Japan, signing a treaty in 1858, Japanese art work had a great influence, and although the crafts revival in the 1880s was not primarily concerned with jewellery it paved the way for forward-looking designers well aware of what was going on in Europe.

Opposite: C. R. Ashbee (1863 - 1942) was perhaps the most influential figure in design of his day, the principal organiser of the Arts and Crafts movement, and a designer in many materials. Widely known abroad by his distinctive work, he eventually lost faith in Arts and Crafts and hand-made products and was a pioneer advocate of the machine made. This brooch c. 1900 was silver with wire work, pearls, and a variety of gemstones.

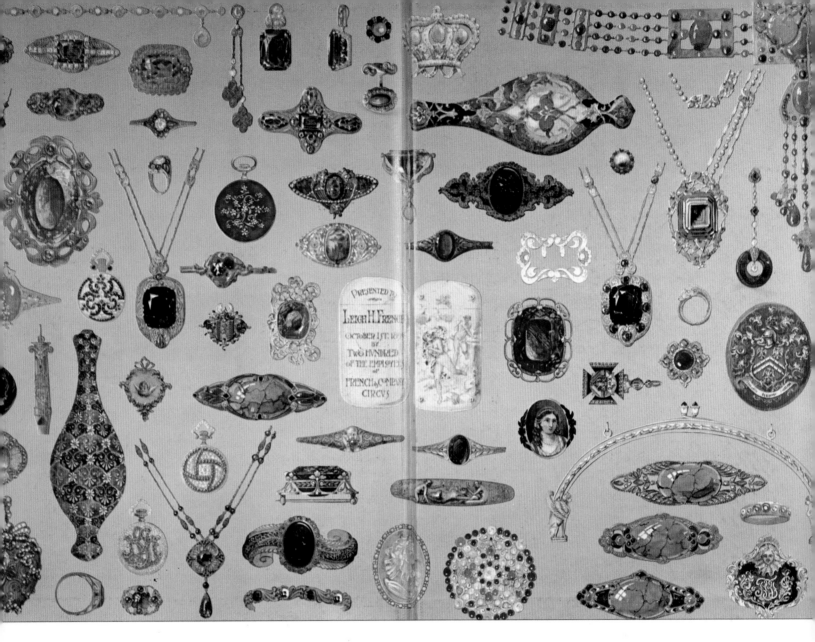

American art nouveau jewellery was dominated by Louis Comfort Tiffany (1848 – 1933), who formed an interior decorating firm in 1878. Best known for his glass, Tiffany regarded what he called his "art" jewellery as immensely important, but realised, as his contemporaries in Britain and Europe did not, that it was for an elite and would be too expensive and obscure for the masses. In Britain a watered-down art nouveau was provided for the many, spasmodically, almost shamefacedly, but in America commercial art nouveau jewellery was produced on a large scale in Newark, New Jersey, and Providence, Rhode Island (the Gorham Corporation Inc had been established as early as 1815). Gorham's jewellery was called Martele, from the French word meaning hammered, and was centred on metalwork, with few stones, though agates and pearls were used. It was bold and stylish, craft-orientated, though the "art" jewellery was influenced more by Paris than London. Ingenious methods were used to give mass-production jewellery the appearance of opulence. "Jewels" were stamped out of metal, and some of the pieces were quite large.

Where America excelled was in promoting their products, and in utilising current fads. The celebrated Gibson Girl was turned into a brooch in 1903 with the fetching title "Flor-a-Dora", though it was only a variation on the now traditional art nouveau lady with flowing tresses. The better jewellery of the period was openly indebted to

Above: A double page of jewellery from the Tiffany catalogue of 1890, some of the items admittedly rather dull.

Opposite: A selection of diverse nineteenth-century jewellery, some art nouveau, some Victorian verging into art nouveau, the cameo brooch being typically sedate Victorian. Whn not being pompous, Victorian jewellery before the age of art nouveau could be surprisingly adventurous and frivolous.

Left: A Victorian butterfly brooch, a black opal, a black opal ring, three unmounted opals, a black opal pendant and ring, and a gem-set butterfly brooch.

France, except for the unique contribution of Tiffany, who was himself influenced by Lalique. Tiffany's own work was decried in Paris for its lack of artistry, His use of the peacock motif was perhaps influenced by the British jewellery designer C. R. Ashbee, who visited his studios in America, but Oriental and Byzantine motifs appear again and again. He used pearls, unusual gems such as a green garnet, gold as a fluid tactile material, and rich enamels. Unlike his glass, Tiffany's jewellery was not a commercial success, and on the whole the art nouveau period affected America far less than Britain and Europe.

As we can see from British advertisements and trade catalogues of the time, the major chain stores sold jewellery with an echo of art nouveau, but with the price of diamonds low the emphasis was on glitter and sometimes the merging of the traditional show jewellery and art nouveau is disastrous. Rivals sometimes imitated Liberty jewellery unashamedly; the best known is the firm of Murrle Bennett, though there is a suspicion, as Murrle Bennett was started earlier, that Liberty at times copied them. Murrle Bennett had its own team of inspired designers. Murrle Bennett did not have a retail outlet in Regent Street in London, as Liberty did, and remained very much in the twilight.

Art nouveau jewellery was less important to most people than art nouveau architecture, book design, furniture, silver, and decorative metal work. It was largely impractical, cheap imitations showed their lineage, and the clever intricacy was often unobserved when the jewellery was worn. It was created by the few for the few. In the end it was a fine art, not an applied art.

Opposite: Although an enamel and gold watch made by the firm of Leroy et Fils, the casing in a ladybird shape certainly qualifies the piece as jewellery.

Below: A sapphire and diamond ring by Tiffany, a 9.96 carat diamond ring by Petochi, and a ruby and diamond ring.

ART DECO AND AFTER

If there is a word to describe Art Deco jewellery it might be brutalist, though this would ignore the work done by the elderly jewellers who had developed their art during the art nouveau period hardly more than 20 years before and who still favoured gentle curves and sinuous shapes, though Lalique adopted his style to the new era.

If Art Deco had not existed, it would have to be invented. Nothing mirrors the revolution in social attitudes, in perceptions, in morals and countless other spheres that followed the break up of traditional civilization caused by World War I as much as Art Deco. There was also a wholehearted acceptance of the machine age and its products, at its most ludicrous in the Vorticist art movement. .

Yet there is a paradox, for along with the brutalism there was elegance. Geometric shapes could be beautiful, and the Art Deco movement encompassed every aspect of applied art – architecture, furniture, ceramics, glass, book design, and industrial design.

Jewellery gave the impression of being machine-made even when it was not, but crafted by outstanding designers, mainly French, such as Sandoz, Templier, Fouquet and Brandt. If there was a connection with art nouveau it is that quintessential Art Deco was intended for the few, though the designs filtered down to the mass of the public, especially in furniture, ceramics, and household appliances.

The name Art Deco was only one of a number of candidates for the wholly novel way of looking at things. It is derived from the *Exposition Internationale des Artes Decoratifs et Industriels*

Above: An Art Deco emerald and diamond pendant.

Opposite: A pair of cacti brooches, an Art Deco vanity case, an Art Deco sapphire and diamond suite, a sapphire ring, and a sapphire and diamond ring.

Above: A brooch by Salvador Dali (1904 - 1989) entitled "The Eye of Time", rather less surrealist than one would have anticipated.

Modernes of 1925, and was popularised in the 1960s especially by the first serious writer on the subject, Bevis Hillier.

Inspiration was drawn from Oriental art, the Aztec and Mayan civilizations, art movements such as Cubism, Vorticism, and Futurism, Russian ballet, ethnic artifacts, native America, and ancient Egypt following the discovery in 1922 of Tutankhamun's tomb. The lotus flower and the scarab were constantly recurring motifs. But above all, there were geometric shapes, often tortured into a strange solemnity, and one wonders, as with some art nouveau jewellery, if this was ever worn or if these pieces were miniature art objects.

Much jewellery which was actually worn, known since 1910 as *bijou de couture*, was far more conventional and designed for Chanel and Schiaparelli, with rhinestone, a diamond-like gem, much used. The characteristic piece of jewellery was the *sautoir*, a long necklace ending in a pendant. Produced at every price level was the double clip which could be used as a brooch or a dress shoulder clip. The *lavalliere* was a pendant with two clusters hanging from chains of different length.

In all types of jewellery there was an eagerness to experiment with as many materials as possible, often in the same piece, and there was a wide range of plastics available, which were not regarded as a

Opposite: A selection of jewellery including a lady's Art Deco diamond bracelet watch, an amethyst and diamond heart-shaped brooch pendant, a late-Victorian diamond fleur de lis brooch, and a diamond-set jabot (frill on a bodice) pin.

Overleaf~: A silver and malachite brooch, a gold brooch, an enamelled ceramic pendant, and a silver-gilt and enamel pendant, all by Josef Hoffman and Lily Jacobsen.

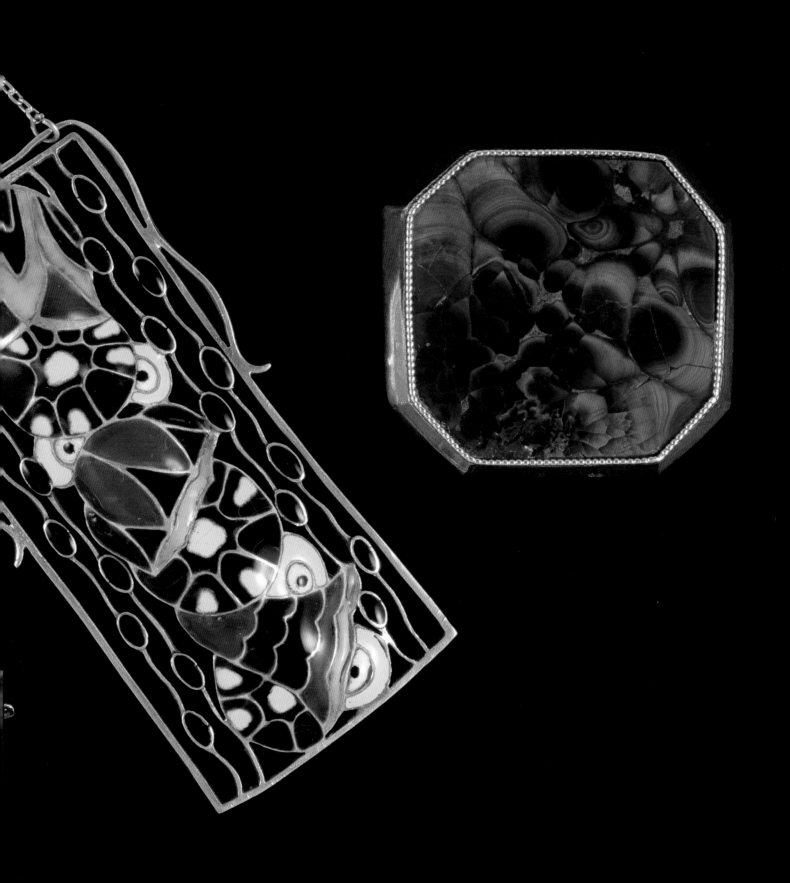

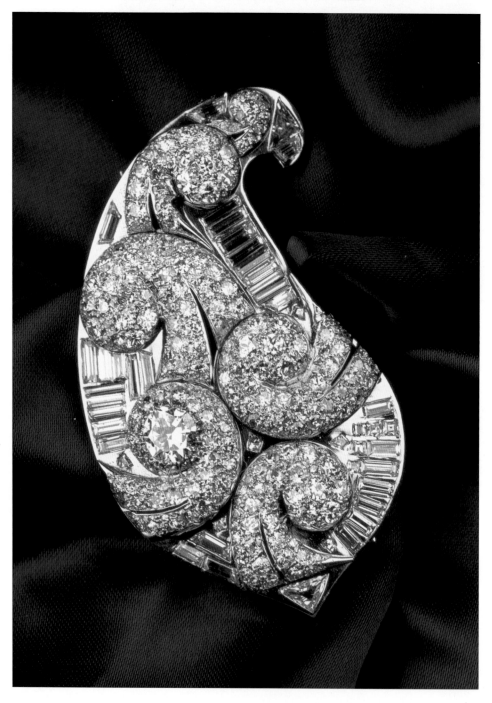

Above: An Art Deco diamond brooch.

Opposite: A display of pendants and brooches made by Heinrich Levinger.

substitute but as marvellous substances in their own right, which of course they were and are. They were often combined with precious stones, silver, and gold. In sharp contrast with art nouveau was the taste for monochrome – black, white, and greys. Silver and platinum were therefore much preferred to gold, and the blacks were supplied by jet, lacquer, or enamel. Diamonds were used, but they were regarded no more highly than rock crystal, used either polished or frosted.

Famous jewellers such as Cartier transcended the medium and accessories such as cigarette cases and powder compacts could also be art works wrought with as much skill as jewellery. There was also a vogue for novelties reflecting newsworthy subjects such as Mickey Mouse, and these could be worn alongside the most sumptuous creations in silver and emeralds. The jewellery made for the mass market was often every bit as impressive as the expensive pieces, as the materials were cheap and mass production could replicate the endeavours of the major jewelers. Without close examination there was no way of knowing which was cheap and which was dear. Although there were social divides, a working-class flapper could deck herself out with all the bravura and conviction of those in the upper echelons.

There is no question that France was the predominant influence on American Art Deco jewellery, though firms such as Tiffany, Udall and Ballou, Spaulding-Gorham and Peacock produced jewellery of a particularly American kind. But American Art Deco is best represented by its cars, its architecture and its household appliances. The supreme achievement of America during the 1920s and 1930s was streamlining. The influence through the continent of Europe of Art Deco was patchy, though Hitler brought the brutalist element to a fever pitch. The lightning flashes on the uniform of the SS are classic Art Deco motifs.

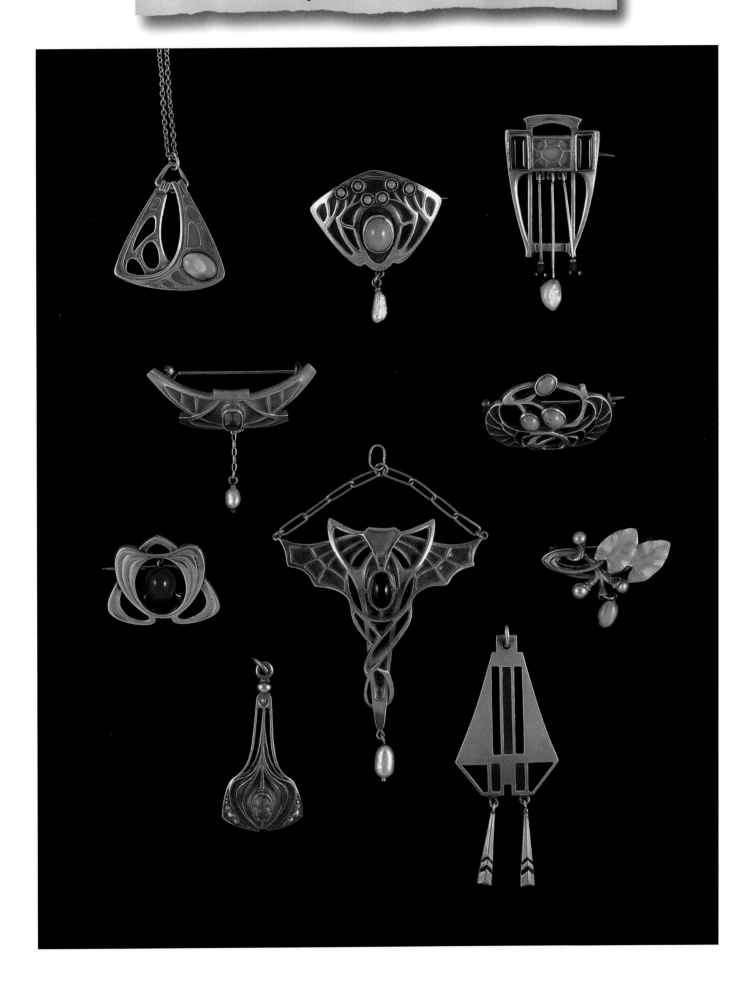

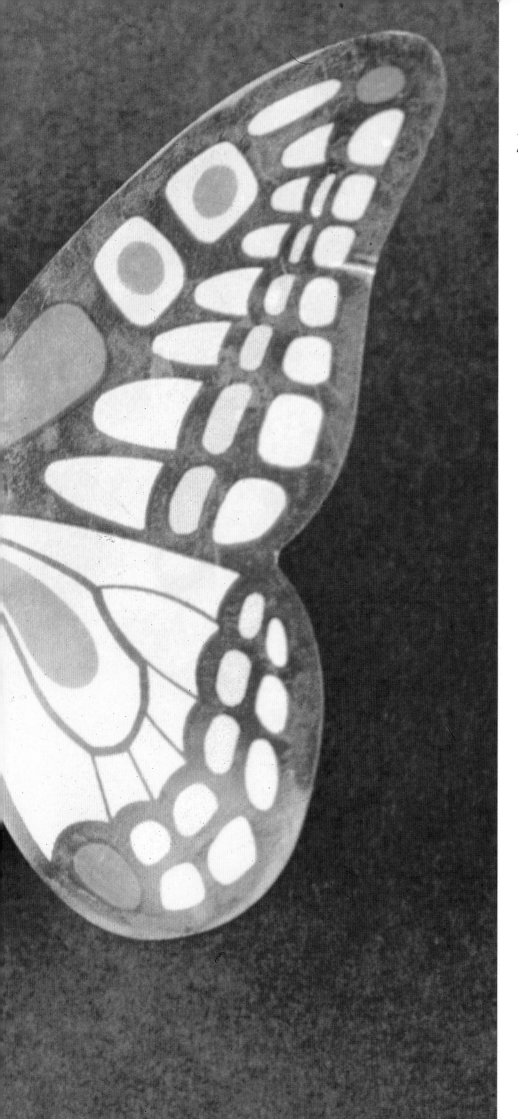

Left: A realistic and colourful butterfly, always a popular theme for jewellery.

After World War II there was no great stylistic adventure, and when the New Look appeared in 1947 there was no upsurge in jewellery design to complement it. Nor has there been any dominant style since, though the Italians have established a strong individual type of jewellery. The accent has largely been on casual jewellery of an ethnic or hippie style, usually hand-made, often lumpy, though costume jewellery has mostly been traditional in taste and appearance except for one-off pieces made to order by the rich and the famous. A glance into the average High Street jeweller's window will not arouse any frisson of excitement.

The market for male jewellery has been greatly increased, with a resurgence of the vogue for large finger rings, ear rings, studs, and bracelets, worn, of course, by women as well, a reminder that human nature alters little over the millennia and such body decoration would go unremarked in early civilizations.

All jewellery is centred around how people think of themselves – as strutting oafs weighed down with gold, as respectable matrons loaded with gems and pearls to establish their social credentials, or as beauties for whom jewellery adds the final touch. The symbolical aspect of jewellery has long been lost, even if vestiges linger in the subconscious. The urge for self-adornment may be a basic human instinct. Or it may not.

Above: A gem-set Art Deco dragonfly brooch.

Opposite: A diamond double-clip brooch, a diamond necklace, and a diamond bracelet, all from the Art Deco period. Because of the nature of the material designers were restricted, and Art Deco diamond jewellery was often almost traditional.

INDEX

PICTURE CREDITS